······················· *Praise for*

Ann Boroch & Her Books

"*The Candida Cure Cookbook* provides a wide array of recipes that are incredibly delicious and fulfill all the important criteria for being healthful. Let food be *your* medicine with these empowering dishes! . . . Ann Boroch's firsthand personal experience coupled with extensive research offers hope to countless undiagnosed and inappropriately treated candida patients."
—DAVID PERLMUTTER, MD, #1 *New York Times* best-selling author of *Grain Brain* and *Brain Maker*

"Yeast and fungus don't stand a fighting chance with *The Candida Cure Cookbook* as your guide. The delectable dishes are not only tasty but offer up immune-enhancing herbs and spices to kick candida to the curb!"—ANN LOUISE GITTLEMAN, PHD, CNS, *New York Times* best-selling author of *The Fat Flush Plan*

"Ann Boroch's nutritional program for overcoming chronic yeast infection is thorough, comprehensive, and effective. The recipes are excellent!"
—LEO GALLAND, MD, author of *The Allergy Solution*

"A woman who's done something really incredible."
—MONTEL WILLIAMS on *The Montel Williams Show*

"[*The Candida Cure* is] a fantastic guide for anyone seeking optimal health and vitality."—GABRIELLE BERNSTEIN, *New York Times* best-selling author of *May Cause Miracles*

"I am very impressed by what Ann Boroch has been doing and continues to do."
—WILLIAM G. CROOK, MD, author of *The Yeast Connection*

The
CANDIDA
CURE
COOKBOOK

The
CANDIDA
CURE
COOKBOOK

Delicious Recipes to Reset Your Health

Restore Your Vitality

ANN BOROCH, CNC

Quintessential Healing Publishing, Inc.

NEW YORK

For information, contact:

Quintessential Healing Publishing, Inc.
www.QuintessentialHealing.com
www.annboroch.com

For foreign and translation rights, contact Nigel J. Yorwerth
Email: nigel@publishingcoaches.com

Library of Congress Control Number: 2015918250

ISBN: 978-0-9773446-6-6 (paperback)
ISBN: 978-0-9773446-7-3 (ebook)

Photographs © Bobak Radbin
Cover and interior design: Nita Ybarra

This book is intended to serve only as a resource and educational guide. This book and the ideas, recipes, programs, and suggestions within are not intended as a substitute for the medical advice of physicians. The reader should regularly consult a physician in matters relating to his/her health and particularly with respect to any symptoms that may require diagnosis or medical attention. Neither the author nor the publisher is engaged in rendering professional advice or services to the reader. All matters regarding health require medical supervision. Women who are pregnant or nursing should consult with their health-care practitioners prior to starting any of the programs discussed in this book. Pregnant and nursing women should not do the 90-day candida-cure program. The author and the publisher shall not be liable for and specifically disclaim any loss, injury, or damage allegedly arising from any information or suggestions in this book. The author and publisher are also not responsible for the reader's specific health or allergy needs that may require medical supervision or for any adverse reactions to the recipes or products contained in this book. It is the reader's responsibility to ensure his or her own health and medical needs are met.

To all those in search of
solutions for living a healthy,
thriving life

Contents

The Healing Power of Your Food

....

THE CANDIDA CURE COOKBOOK was born out of my passion to help people restore their health and vitality by tackling a condition that is at the core of many health problems—candida, or yeast and fungal, overgrowth. *The Candida Cure Cookbook* is filled with delicious sugar-free, dairy-free, gluten-free, and yeast-free recipes that avoid foods that create inflammation and feed candida. Although the recipes are designed for those on an anti-candida diet, anyone who wants to eat clean, whole foods, experience more energy, lose weight, and stay energetic and healthy, even as they age, will benefit from this book.

As more and more research is revealing, candida is a key factor in a wide range of health problems, from allergies, irritable bowel syndrome, leaky gut, sinusitis, fatigue, eczema, and endocrine imbalances to anxiety, depression, brain fog, and autoimmune disease. Significantly, candida and its by-products (mycotoxins) can foster the environment for cancer viruses to flourish. Millions are suffering with an overgrowth of yeast in their bodies and don't even know it.

I'm dedicated to providing solutions to the growing candida epidemic because I've experienced firsthand what can happen when candida gets out of control. Discovering this condition in my own body literally saved my life. In the years since, the candida program and diet I've developed have supported my clients and readers in charting their own road to renewed health. If you've tried different approaches to healing a persistent health issue without success, or if you just can't seem to lose weight or don't have enough energy to get through the day, the candida-cure diet could be the answer for you. Here's a little background on how this book came to be.

At the age of nineteen, I had a severe case of mononucleosis (Epstein–Barr virus). For months, I experienced overwhelming fatigue, disorientation, brain fog, allergies, chest constriction, ear and sinus pain, weight loss, dizziness, and depression. As my condition worsened, I sought more medical treatments. I saw over eight different specialists and took more than twenty different medications.

I felt like a human guinea pig. When nothing worked, I began to search for answers on my own and found Dr. William Crook's first book, *The Yeast Connection*. He was the second doctor, in addition to Dr. Orian Truss, who exposed the link between yeast/candida overgrowth and a variety of health conditions. I cried when I answered the questionnaire in his book because I had 90 percent of the symptoms he listed that are connected with candida. I followed his protocol for an anti-candida diet, avoiding foods that encourage yeast to grow, and took an antifungal powder called Nilstat. Within one year, I was healthy and thriving again.

Unfortunately I didn't understand how important it was, given the severity of my case, to stick to that diet to prevent the yeast from returning even more virulently. My old habit of eating sugars and refined carbohydrates crept back in. On top of that, my stress levels were high, which elevates cortisol and blood sugar, feeding candida. At twenty-four, my world stopped when I experienced a major attack on my neurological system. I couldn't breathe, swallow, or move for seconds and then had uncontrollable spasms and pronounced fatigue. I was quickly diagnosed with multiple sclerosis and told my condition was "incurable."

I refused to accept the doctor's devastating verdict. Once again I dug up what little research was available at the time and was determined to create my own self-care program. It was a tumultuous four-year journey. During that time, I addressed the real factor that was underlying my condition (candida overgrowth), removed fifteen silver-mercury amalgam fillings, and religiously stuck to a diet to fight candida. I took Nystatin tablets, herbal antifungals, and additional supplementation. And I did my inner work by examining and healing mental and emotional wounds.

I have now been symptom-free for over twenty years. My healing journey ignited in me a passion to educate and inspire others to achieve optimal health in the face of any condition. I decided to get trained in several healing disciplines. As a certified nutritionist and naturopath for the last eighteen years and the author of two books, I have helped thousands regain their health and vitality. Those successes are based on teaching people how to get their bodies back into balance and how to target what creates inflammation and infection, including what we eat and drink. Over time, I developed a program of diet, detoxification, and supplementation aimed at eliminating inflammation and allowing the body's innate intelligence to do what it does best—heal.

The Candida Cure Cookbook is a companion to my popular book *The Candida Cure: Yeast, Fungus, and Your Health—The 90-Day Program to Beat Candida and Restore Vibrant Health*. That book offers additional information on treating candida and can guide you in implementing a 90-day program of detox and diet. After hearing from clients and readers that they wanted more recipes so they could maintain the candida-cure diet, I realized that it was time to create a cookbook. There are many allergy-free cookbooks that cater to those on restricted diets but few that deal specifically with candida. And the recipes my clients had found weren't very exciting or tasty. I knew from my own experience that, contrary to what many people think, it is entirely possible to prepare healthy, clean, candida-free food that is mouthwatering too.

Rest assured, *The Candida Cure Cookbook* will not let you down. It is chock full of wholesome, flavorful recipes that will help you beat candida and satisfy your palate. In creating these recipes, I collaborated with chef Alison Charbonneau, the perfect person to make this cookbook come to life. She specializes in cooking for those with restricted diets and compromised immune systems. Alison is talented and creative and she makes irresistible dishes that are tasty, easy to make, and nutritious.

Before you dive into the recipes, I invite you to read through the pages that follow to get familiar with the key principles behind my anti-candida diet and to learn some handy tips for preparing these meals and stocking your pantry. First, you'll see a section on the candida epidemic that explores the causes, symptoms, and solutions to candida overgrowth, including a questionnaire to assist you in determining if candida is a problem for you. Please note that a low questionnaire score does not mean candida is not an issue for you. If you aren't feeling healthy, candida is most likely a factor. You'll also find lists of foods to eat and avoid, tips for shopping and food preparation, and recommended products, tools, and equipment.

Because it can be challenging to stick to an anti-candida diet, I made sure to include a sample four-week menu plan as well. Following that are the more than 140 recipes for nutritious and delicious breakfasts, dressings, dips, sauces, main dishes, side dishes, soups, salads, breads, snacks, beverages, and, last but not least, delectable desserts—all sugar-free, dairy-free, gluten-free, and yeast-free. With all these tips, guidelines, and recipes, *The Candida Cure Cookbook* will help you nourish your body, add variety to your meals, and discover that eating healthy can taste great. I look forward to hearing about your successes.

Enjoy in good health!

ANN BOROCH

Candida and Your Health

························

MANY OF THE MOST COMMON symptoms and illnesses that plague us today—from fatigue, bloating, and weight gain to prostatitis, brain fog, arthritis, allergies, depression, and multiple sclerosis—can be traced back to a surprising source: yeast.

Candida, or yeast, overgrowth is epidemic today and affects millions. Conservatively speaking, one in three people suffers from yeast-related symptoms or conditions. While women immediately associate candida with vaginal yeast infections, men hear the word *fungus* and think it's the problem they're having with their toenails. But it's much more.

In addition to the conditions I've already named, candida is associated with persistent symptoms like ear and sinus problems, upper respiratory infections, PMS, fibroids, endometriosis, hypothyroidism, hypoglycemia, acne, and anxiety as well as more severe conditions such as auto-immune diseases, fibromyalgia, lupus, autism, mental illness, and even cancer.

How can yeast be such a significant health factor when so many don't even know about it? Simply because Western medicine continues to quietly ignore the connection between yeast overgrowth and the overuse of prescription drugs, especially antibiotics, and other common offenders, including diet and even the air we breathe.

WHAT IS CANDIDA?

Candida albicans is a harmless yeast, a type of fungus, that lives naturally in everyone's body: male, female, and child alike. In a healthy body, it lives symbiotically in a balanced environment in the gastrointestinal tract, on the mucous membranes, and on the skin. Unfortunately, this harmless yeast can overgrow and turn into an opportunistic pathogen.

As Dr. Michael Goldberg states: "Because it is a commensal organism [one that benefits from another organism without damaging or benefiting it] present in virtually all human beings from birth, it is ideally positioned to take immediate advantage of any weakness or debility in the host, and probably has few equals in the variety and severity of the infections for which it is responsible."[1]

Candida overgrowth and its by-products, mycotoxins, can attack any organ or system in your body. The attack is relentless, twenty-four hours a day, until treated. If not arrested, yeast, a single-celled organism, will change form—into a pathogenic fungus with roots that causes myriad symptoms.

Throughout this section, I will be using the words *yeast* and *fungus* interchangeably. This fungus burrows its roots into the intestinal lining and creates leaky gut—increased intestinal permeability— which allows the fungus and its by-products to escape into the bloodstream. According to an article in the journal *Science*, "*Candida albicans* is the most common human systemic pathogen, causing both mucosal and systemic infections, particularly in immunocompromised people."[2] A systemic fungal infection is called candidiasis.

LIFESTYLE FACTORS THAT ENCOURAGE CANDIDA OVERGROWTH

The major causes of *Candida albicans* overgrowth are antibiotics, steroids (e.g., cortisone and prednisone), birth control pills, estrogen replacement therapy, poor diet, chemotherapy, radiation, heavy metals, alcohol overuse, recreational drugs, and stress. Other contributing factors include heavy metals in our silver amalgam fillings and the lead and cadmium in polluted air. All of the above directly or indirectly destroy the good bacteria in our gastrointestinal tract, allowing yeast to take over.

Yeast overgrowth thrives in the presence of diets high in refined sugars, refined carbohydrates, dairy products, alcohol, processed foods, and hormones secreted as a result of high stress levels. Acute stress and chronic stress elevate cortisol, a hormone produced by the adrenal glands (small glands that sit on top of each kidney). Excessive cortisol, in turn, raises blood sugar. The fungus doesn't care whether the increased sugar in your body is due to eating a candy bar or to having an episode of extreme stress; it will use the sugar as fuel to reproduce itself.

Once an imbalance occurs, yeast continues to multiply as it is fed by sugar in any form—alcohol, desserts, white flour, dairy products such as milk and cheese, and elevated sugar levels caused by high stress. As years go by, mild to severe health conditions appear.

It is easy to see why the incidence of candidiasis is so high—the main contributing factors are various mainstream Western medicine protocols, rampant poor diet, and the stress overload so prevalent in our society today.

Western medicine may deny that yeast causes these myriad conditions, but the truth is that fungal toxins—the by-products produced by the yeast—disrupt cellular communication. Once that happens, inflammation and infection settle wherever we are genetically weak.

It takes only one dose of antibiotics in your lifetime to raise your yeast levels and create imbalances in your body. If you last took a course of antibiotics when you were ten years old, a poor diet and high stress levels will continue to feed the yeast over time until you begin to feel symptomatic.

North America, especially the United States and Canada, and pockets of Europe, have the highest numbers of people with candidiasis because Western medicine's standard protocol is to use antibiotic therapy for common infections.

A vicious cycle starts with the use of antibiotics. For example, you have a cold or the flu and you visit your doctor, who prescribes antibiotics. The problem starts right there because colds and flu are viral infections, not bacterial ones, which is what antibiotics are designed for. Antibiotics are useless against colds and flu, yet many doctors prescribe them anyway. When you take the antibiotic it kills both good and bad bacteria in your gastrointestinal tract, as it cannot distinguish between them. Antibiotics do not affect *Candida albicans*, so without friendly bacteria like *Lactobacillus acidophilus* and *Bifidobacteria*, which keep the *Candida albicans* under control, the candida now multiplies.

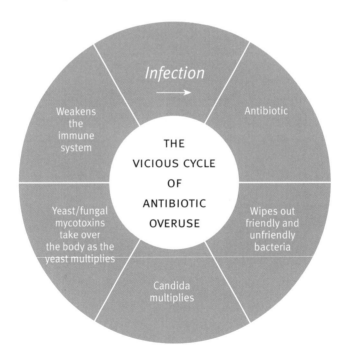

SOURCE: Content reprinted courtesy of William G. Crook, MD, *The Yeast Connection Handbook* (Jackson, TN: Professional Books, 2000). Used with permission.

There is no question that antibiotics have saved thousands of lives, but we've pushed a good thing too far by overprescribing these medications. Overuse also creates "super germs" that are resistant to common antibiotics, so germs that could once be killed off have now become life threatening.

As I mentioned, it takes only one dose of antibiotics to raise your yeast levels. Think about how many times you've taken antibiotics—not to mention the antibiotics you ingest from consuming dairy and animal products. The majority of antibiotics manufactured today are given to cows and chickens because they are infested with infection due to their poor housing conditions. So unless you are eating antibiotic-free and hormone-free animal protein, you are ingesting these drugs and hormones when you eat these foods.

CANDIDA'S TOXIC BY-PRODUCTS

Once candida is in an overgrowth state, the body has to deal not only with the overgrowth but also with the toxic by-products, or mycotoxins, that *Candida albicans* puts out—"79 at latest count,"[3] according to C. Orian Truss, MD—all of which weaken your immune system and attack the body. Mycotoxins are neurotoxins that destroy and decompose tissues and organs. They are so powerful that they upset the very communication of cell interactions, disrupt RNA and DNA synthesis, damage and destroy neurons, are carcinogenic, and cause ataxia (lack of coordination) and even convulsions. These pernicious yeast toxins confuse body systems, which accounts for the cross-wiring problems of the immune system whereby the body attacks itself, as in those with autoimmune diseases.

Candida toxins commonly get through the gut lining when it becomes leaky and enter the blood-stream, where the liver can detoxify them. However, if the liver's detoxification ability is impaired due to inadequate nutrition and toxic overload, these toxins will settle in other organs and tissues, such as the brain, nervous system, joints, skin, and so forth. Over time, chronic disease will occur.

One of the major toxins produced from *Candida albicans* is acetaldehyde (a by-product of alcohol metabolism), which the liver converts into a harmless substance. However, if there is an excess of acetaldehyde and the liver becomes oversaturated, it is released into the bloodstream, creating feelings of intoxication, brain fog, vertigo, and loss of equilibrium. Acetaldehyde alters the structure of red blood cells and compromises the transportation pathways whereby materials are delivered to feed the dendrites (nerve cell extensions), which causes the dendrites to atrophy and die off. In addition, acetaldehyde creates a deficiency of thiamine (vitamin B1), a vitamin that is critical for brain and nerve function and essential for the production of acetylcholine, one of the brain's major neurotransmitters (see the chart below). This deficiency brings on emotional apathy, depression, fatigue, insomnia, confusion, and memory loss.

DAMAGE FROM ACETALDEHYDE

Acetaldehyde Damages Brain Function

- Impaired memory
- Decreased ability to concentrate ("brain fog")
- Depression
- Slowed reflexes
- Lethargy and apathy
- Heightened irritability
- Decreased mental energy

- Increased anxiety and panic
- Decreased sensory acuity
- Increased tendency to alcohol and sugar
- Decreased sex drive
- Increased PMS and breast swelling/tenderness in women

SOURCE: James A. South MA, *Vitamin Research Products Nutritional News*, July 1997.

Acetaldehyde also depletes niacin (vitamin B3), which is key to helping the cells burn fat and sugar for energy. Niacin plays an important role in the production of serotonin, a neurotransmitter that affects mood and sleep, and in producing a coenzyme that breaks down alcohol. In addition, acetaldehyde reduces enzymes in the body that help to produce energy in all cells, including brain cells.

Gliotoxin, another mycotoxin, deactivates important enzymes that move toxins through the body and also causes DNA changes in the white blood cells, which suppresses the immune system. As your immune system continues to weaken from fungus and mycotoxins, more infections arise, and you end up at the doctor's office again—being prescribed more antibiotics and perpetuating the vicious cycle.

CANDIDA'S PREFERRED TARGETS

Candida albicans primarily targets the nerves and muscles, yet it can attack any tissue or organ, depending on your body's genetic predisposition (see the list on page 9). Mild symptoms of yeast overgrowth are fatigue, gas, bloating, heartburn, brain fog, weight gain, constipation, arthritic pain, sinus infections, high and low blood sugar, allergies, depression, and anxiety. More severe conditions can eventually develop, including autoimmune diseases and cancer.

To understand how candida penetrates through your system, think of your body as having two skins of protection that keep out foreign invaders. One is the outside skin and the other is your inside skin, which starts in your nasal passages and runs all the way down to your rectum. This tissue is the same from top to bottom, and if it becomes inflamed or irritated, the membranes become more porous, allowing foreign invaders to enter the bloodstream. In the journal *Infection and Immunity*, Michael J. Kennedy and Paul A. Volz explain, "The passage of viable *Candida albicans* through the gastrointestinal (GI) mucosa into the bloodstream is believed to be an important mechanism leading to systemic candidosis."[4]

YEAST/FUNGAL OVERGROWTH *Conditions caused directly or indirectly by overgrowth*

Autoimmune Diseases
ALS (Lou Gehrig's Disease)
Celiac Disease
Crohn's Disease
Hashimoto's Thyroiditis
HIV/AIDS
Lupus
Multiple Sclerosis
Muscular Dystrophy
Myasthenia Gravis
Psoriasis
Rheumatoid Arthritis
Sarcoidosis
Scleroderma
Sjögren's Syndrome
Ulcerative Colitis
Vitiligo

Blood System
Chronic Infections
Iron Deficiency
Thrombocytopenic Purpura

Cancer

Cardiovascular
Endocarditis
Pericarditis
Mitral Valve Prolapse
Valve Problems

Digestive System
Anorexia Nervosa
Bloating/Gas

Carbohydrate/Sugar
  Cravings
Colitis
Constipation/Diarrhea
Dysbiosis
Food Allergies
Gastritis
Heartburn
Intestinal Pain
Irritable Bowel Syndrome
Leaky Gut
Malabsorption/Maldigestion
Pancreatitis
SIBO

Musculoskeletal System
Arthritis
Fibromyalgia
Gout

Skin
Acne
Athletes' Foot
Diaper Rash
Dry Skin and Itching
Eczema
Hives
Hair Loss
Jock Itch
Leprosy
Liver Spots
Toenail Fungus

**Respiratory System/
Ears/Eyes/Mouth**
Asthma
Bronchitis
Dizziness
Earaches
Environmental Allergies/
  Chemical Sensitivities
Hay Fever
Meniere's Disease
Oral Thrush
Sinusitis

Endocrine System
Adrenal/Thyroid Failure
Chronic Fatigue Syndrome
Diabetes
Hormonal Imbalances
Hypoglycemia
Insomnia
Over/Underweight
PCOS

Nervous System
Alcoholism
Alzheimer's Disease
Anxiety
Attention Deficit Disorder
Autism
Brain Fog
Depression
Headaches
Hyperactivity

Hyperirritability
Learning Difficulties
Manic-Depressive Disorder
Memory Loss
Migraines
Schizophrenia
Suicidal Tendencies
Trigeminal Neuralgia

Urinary/Reproductive
Bladder Infections
Endometriosis
Fibroids
Impotence
Infertility
Interstitial Cystitis
Loss of Libido
Menstrual Irregularities
PMS
Prostatitis
Sexually Transmitted
  Diseases
Urethritis
Vaginal Yeast Infections

Viruses
Epstein-Barr Virus
Herpes
Human Papillomavirus
Shingles

Cellular disruption occurs when *Candida albicans* and its mycotoxins have accumulated in the body. This disruption causes secondary body systems to deteriorate. Mycotoxins so severely debilitate the body that "victims could become easy prey for far more serious diseases such as acquired immune deficiency syndrome, multiple sclerosis, rheumatoid arthritis, myasthenia gravis, colitis, regional ileitis, schizophrenia, and possibly death from candida septicemia," say Kennedy and Volz.[5] Your genetic weaknesses usually determine which system or organs will be affected.

SETTING OFF A CASCADE OF IMBALANCES

Candida overgrowth creates a cascade of imbalances in the body. Three major areas worth noting are the proliferation of other microorganisms, imbalances in the hormonal system, and emotional disturbances, especially anxiety and depression.

Bacteria, Parasites, and Viruses

Unfortunately, once the body's internal environment is out of balance, not only does candida multiply but so do other microorganisms. Why? Because a poor diet and/or high stress levels elevate blood sugar in the body, which in turn feeds bacteria, parasites, and viruses. One of the most common viral infections, Epstein-Barr virus, also known as mononucleosis, cannot surface without the presence of yeast overgrowth. Therefore, when treating candida, I suggest using a broad-spectrum antimicrobial herbal remedy that addresses not only yeast and fungus but bacteria, parasites, and viruses as well.

Endocrine Imbalances

Candida overgrowth indirectly impacts the functioning of the endocrine system, which releases hormones that regulate the body's metabolic activity. The endocrine system consists of the hypothalamus, pituitary, thyroid, thymus, adrenals, pancreas, and ovaries or testes.

Problems related to these glands and organs include low blood sugar (hypoglycemia), diabetes, and obesity, all of which are increasing at alarming proportions in the United States. Hypothyroidism is rampant, especially among women. And the ailment most common across the board with males and females is adrenal exhaustion, where the adrenals output chronically high cortisol levels, resulting in fatigue, low immunity, anxiety, insomnia, and weight gain.

The primary aggravators of these conditions are a poor diet, consisting of refined carbohydrates and sugar, and unmanaged stress. The secondary aggravator is yeast overgrowth.

Over the years, I have had many clients say to me, "Why can't I lose weight? I'm eating healthy foods and exercising and can't drop a pound." The missing link is clearing the body of infection by getting rid of candida overgrowth, which eliminates inflammation and allows the body systems to normalize. Eradicate candida and watch the inches and pounds drop as your endocrine system comes back into balance.

Emotional and Mental Imbalances

Depression and anxiety are widespread and can, in part, be related to chronic yeast overgrowth in the tissues. The reason, as described by J. P. Nolan in an article in the journal *Hepatology*, is the link between the gut and the brain: "An individual's ability to protect against brain-active substances depends upon the status of his or her intestinal flora, GI mucosal function and hepatic (liver) detoxification ability."[6] This means that when leaky gut is present and the liver is overstressed, the door is open for toxins to reach the brain via the bloodstream.

Unfortunately, too many physicians assume that all mental and emotional imbalances have psychological causes, such as neuroses or psychoses, rather than brain-related causes, as Dr. C. Orian Truss points out in *The Missing Diagnosis*: "I would like to make a special plea that we speak of manifestations of abnormal brain function not as 'mental symptoms' but as 'brain symptoms.' Inherent in the term 'mental symptom' is the connotation that somehow 'the mind' is a separate entity from the brain, that 'mental' symptoms are occurring (at least initially) in a brain that is functioning normally chemically and physiologically. We speak of kidney, liver, or intestinal symptoms when abnormal function manifests itself in these organs, but we use the term 'mental symptoms' rather than 'brain symptoms' when a similar problem occurs with brain physiology."[7]

Having anxiety and/or depression can be debilitating, and it's important to understand that the cause may not be purely psychological but also chemical. Mycotoxins from fungus need to be considered when tackling these conditions. When this is a contributing factor, clearing fungal overgrowth from the system will help clear your mind and bring your body chemistry back into balance.

ACKNOWLEDGING THE REAL PROBLEM

To this day, Western medicine largely does not recognize intestinal and systemic candidiasis as a health condition. Don't be surprised if you take this information to your doctor and he or she dismisses it or tells you that you are crazy. Often doctors only recognize and treat *Candida albicans* overgrowth in cases of oral thrush and vaginal infections or in conditions associated with HIV/AIDS.

With antibiotics, hormone replacement drugs, birth control pills, and steroid drugs accounting for millions of dollars in prescriptions written each year, doctors may find it hard to acknowledge that the drugs they so freely prescribe are actually creating the problem and that intestinal candidiasis even exists. While there are some doctors who will treat intestinal and systemic candidiasis, they are few and far between.

Candida needs to become a household word, recognized for the impact it is having on our health. The good news is that more and more research is supporting the link between candida and a variety of conditions, bringing a rising awareness of what you are learning here—that yeast and fungal overgrowth is the hidden cause of many illnesses and that a diet that avoids foods that fuel candida and that consists of clean, fresh, and wholesome ingredients is key to staying vibrant and healthy.

DO I HAVE CANDIDA?

The questionnaire on the following pages will help you determine whether *Candida albicans* is contributing to your health problems, but it won't provide an automatic yes or no answer. Even if you score low on this test, indicating a lesser possibility of candida, I still recommend that you follow my 90-day program since the typical lifestyle habits of most people today make it almost certain that you have a mild to moderate case of yeast overgrowth. It's challenging to come up with exactly the right test, whether written or in the laboratory, to confirm candida overgrowth. You have nothing to lose, but only a chance to gain more health and vitality by following a candida elimination program.

The questionnaire, developed by William G. Crook, MD, lists factors in your medical history that promote the growth of *Candida albicans* (Section A) as well as symptoms commonly found in individuals with yeast-connected illness (Sections B and C).

Notes

1 Michael J. Goldberg, "Autism and the Immune Connection," www.neuroimmunedr.com/articles.html.

2 Christina M. Hull, Ryan M. Raisner, and Alexander D. Johnson, "Evidence for Mating of the 'Asexual' Yeast *Candida albicans* in a Mammalian Host," *Science* 289, no. 5477 (July 2000).

3 C. Orian Truss, *The Missing Diagnosis* (Birmingham, AL: The Missing Diagnosis, Inc., 1985), 24.

4 Michael J. Kennedy and Paul A. Volz, "Ecology of *Candida albicans* Gut Colonization: Inhibition of Candida Adhesion, Colonization, and Dissemination from the Gastrointestinal Tract by Bacterial Antagonism," *Infection and Immunity*, September 1985, 49(3): 654–63, quoted in John P. Trowbridge and Morton Walker, *The Yeast Syndrome: How to Help Your Doctor Identify and Treat the Real Cause of Your Yeast-Related Illness* (New York: Bantam Books, 1986), 49.

5 Ibid, 9.

6 J. P. Nolan, "Intestinal Endotoxins as Mediators of Hepatic Injury—an Idea Whose Time Has Come Again," *Hepatology* 10, no. 5 (November 1989): 887–91.

7 C. Orian Truss, *The Missing Diagnosis* (Birmingham, AL: The Missing Diagnosis, Inc., 1985), 46.

Candida Health Questionnaire

. . . .

For each "yes" answer in Section A, circle the point score next to the question. Total your score and record it at the end of the section. Then move on to Sections B and C and score as directed. At the end of the questionnaire, you will add your scores to get your grand total.

Section A: History   *Point Score*

1 Have you taken any tetracyclines (Sumycin, Panmycin, Vibramycin, Minocin, etc.) or other antibiotics for acne for one month (or longer)? 50

2 Have you at any time in your life taken other "broad spectrum" antibiotics for respiratory, urinary, or other infections for two months or longer, or for shorter periods four or more times in a one-year span? 50

3 Have you taken an antibiotic drug—even for one round? 6

4 Have you at any time in your life been bothered by persistent prostatitis, vaginitis, or other problems affecting your reproductive organs? 25

5 Have you been pregnant two or more times? 5

   One time? 3

6 Have you taken birth control pills for more than two years? 15

   For six months to two years? 8

7 Have you taken prednisone, Decadron, or other cortisone-type drugs by mouth or inhalation for more than two weeks?* 15

   For two weeks or less? 6

8 Does exposure to perfumes, insecticides, fabric shop odors, or other chemicals provoke moderate to severe symptoms? 20

   Mild symptoms? 5

9 Are your symptoms worse on damp, muggy days or in moldy places? 20

10 Have you had athlete's foot, ringworm, "jock itch," or other chronic fungus infections of the skin or nails?

   Have such infections been severe or persistent? 20

   Mild to moderate? 10

11 Do you crave sugar? 10

12 Do you crave breads? 10

13 Do you crave alcoholic beverages? 10

14 Does tobacco smoke really bother you? 10

Total Score, Section A   _____

*The use of nasal or bronchial sprays containing cortisone and/or other steroids promotes overgrowth in the respiratory tract.

SOURCE: This questionnaire is adapted from William G. Crook, MD, *The Yeast Connection Handbook* (Jackson, TN: Professional Books, Inc., 2000). Used with permission.

Section B: Major Symptoms

For each symptom you experience, enter the appropriate number in the point score column:
- If a symptom is occasional or mild, score 3 points.
- If a symptom is frequent and/or moderately severe, score 6 points.
- If a symptom is severe and/or disabling, score 9 points.

Total the score and record it at the end of this section.

	Point Score
1 Fatigue or lethargy	_____
2 Feeling "drained"	_____
3 Poor memory	_____
4 Feeling "spacey" or "unreal"	_____
5 Inability to make decisions	_____
6 Numbness, burning, or tingling	_____
7 Insomnia	_____
8 Muscle aches	_____
9 Muscle weakness or paralysis	_____
10 Pain and/or swelling in joints	_____
11 Abdominal pain	_____
12 Constipation	_____
13 Diarrhea	_____
14 Bloating, belching, or intestinal gas	_____
15 Troublesome vaginal burning, itching, or discharge	_____
16 Prostatitis	_____
17 Impotence	_____
18 Loss of sexual desire or feeling	_____
19 Endometriosis or infertility	_____
20 Cramps and/or other menstrual irregularities	_____
21 Premenstrual tension	_____
22 Attacks of anxiety or crying	_____
23 Cold hands or feet and/or chilliness	_____
24 Shaking or irritability when hungry	_____

Total Score, Section B _____

Section C: Other Symptoms*

For each symptom you experience, enter the appropriate number in the point score column:
- If a symptom is occasional or mild, score 3 points.
- If a symptom is frequent and/or moderately severe, score 6 points.
- If a symptom is severe and/or disabling, score 9 points.

Total the score and record it at the end of this section.

		Point Score
1	Drowsiness	_____
2	Irritability or jitteriness	_____
3	Lack of coordination	_____
4	Inability to concentrate	_____
5	Frequent mood swings	_____
6	Headaches	_____
7	Dizziness and/or loss of balance	_____
8	Pressure above ears or feeling of head swelling	_____
9	Tendency to bruise easily	_____
10	Chronic rashes or itching	_____
11	Psoriasis or recurrent hives	_____
12	Indigestion or heartburn	_____
13	Food sensitivities or intolerances	_____
14	Mucus in stools	_____
15	Rectal itching	_____
16	Dry mouth or throat	_____
17	Rash or blisters in mouth	_____
18	Bad breath	_____
19	Foot, hair, or body odor not relieved by washing	_____
20	Nasal congestion or postnasal drip	_____
21	Nasal itching	_____
22	Sore throat	_____
23	Laryngitis or loss of voice	_____
24	Cough or recurrent bronchitis	_____
25	Pain or tightness in chest	_____
26	Wheezing or shortness of breath	_____
27	Urinary frequency, urgency, or incontinence	_____
28	Burning on urination	_____
29	Erratic vision or spots in front of eyes	_____
30	Burning or tearing of eyes	_____
31	Recurrent infections or fluid in ears	_____
32	Ear pain or deafness	_____

Total Score, Section C _____

*Although the symptoms in this section occur commonly in patients with yeast-connected illness, they also occur commonly in patients who do not have candida.

Total Score, Section A _____

Total Score, Section B _____

Total Score, Section C _____

Grand Total Score (Add totals from sections A, B, and C) _____

The Grand Total Score will help you and your practitioner decide if your health problems are yeast-connected. Scores for women will run higher because seven items apply exclusively to women, while only two apply exclusively to men.

- Yeast-connected health problems are almost certainly present in women with scores over 180 and in men with scores over 140.
- Yeast-connected health problems are probably present in women with scores over 120 and in men with scores over 90.
- Yeast-connected health problems are possibly present in women with scores over 60 and in men with scores over 40.
- Scores of less than 60 for women and less than 40 for men indicate that yeast are less apt to cause health problems.

Recommended Foods

....

THE FOLLOWING LISTS give you general guidelines about the foods that are beneficial to eat and do not promote the growth of yeast as well as the foods that you need to avoid because they do promote yeast overgrowth. Be aware, however, that everyone's body chemistry is different. Some people have sensitivities or allergies to certain foods on the "Foods to Eat" list, so observe your body in case it reacts negatively to any of the foods.

Symptoms such as fatigue, itching, breathing difficulty, rapid heart rate, gas, burping, bloating, constipation, diarrhea, and headaches are signs that you need to stay away from particular foods. Listen to your body. It will tell you what it wants and does not want. Be aware, though, that when your body is toxic, you are going to crave more of the offending foods. But as you cleanse, your body will start to desire healthier foods and it will be easier to trust the signals that it gives you.

Even though the recipes contain only the recommended foods, these lists will give you an idea of which ingredients are acceptable to use as substitutes and additions and which foods you should avoid.

Foods to Eat

Animal Protein (antibiotic- and hormone-free as much as possible; eat 2–4 ounces once or twice daily or no less than 3 times a week)

Beef, bison, lamb (grass-fed; no more than a 3- to 4-ounce serving once a week; prepare rare to medium-rare and eat with greens and not with starchy vegetables, beans, or grains)

Chicken, duck, and turkey

Eggs (organic or pasture-raised, if possible)

Fish (limit shellfish to once or twice a month)

Note: Due to ongoing ocean pollution from many sources, including nuclear leaks at the Fukushima Daiichi power plant in Japan, stay up to date on which fish become contaminated.

Grains (whole and unrefined only)

Amaranth

Breads (gluten-, yeast-, sugar-, and dairy-free)

Brown rice (short and long grain, brown basmati); brown-rice cakes and crackers; wild rice (limit to 2–3 times a week total)

Buckwheat

Kañiwa

Millet

Oats (gluten-free,* only after 2 months on program)

Pasta (brown-rice, buckwheat, quinoa pasta only; limit to once a week)

Quinoa

Sorghum (can make like popcorn)

Tapioca

Teff

Yucca

Vegetables

All (except corn, mushrooms, peas, and potatoes)

Sweet potatoes, yams, and winter squash (limit to 2–3 servings a week total)

Note: Limit or avoid nightshade-family vegetables for the first 3 months (eggplant, tomatoes, and peppers) because they can cause inflammation. If you eat them and your symptoms increase, avoid completely for the first 3 months and then reintroduce in small amounts if you wish.

Beans and Legumes

You may eat small quantities once or twice a week only or avoid this group entirely for the first 2 months of the program because of their potential to cause inflammation and their high starch levels, which raise blood sugar. If you avoid them and then reintroduce, eat only small amounts once or twice weekly. In either case, do not eat any soy, fermented soy products, or peas. Bragg Liquid Aminos is the only soy product allowed and may be used from the beginning of your program.

Nuts and Seeds (raw; unroasted if commercial; may dry-roast your own)

Almonds

Brazil nuts

Chestnuts

Chia seeds

Flaxseeds

Hazelnuts

Hempseeds

Macadamia nuts

Nut butters (almond and macadamia only; may be raw or dry-roasted)

Pecans

Pine nuts

Pumpkin seeds and pumpkin-seed butter

Sesame seeds (also raw tahini butter)

Sunflower seeds and sunflower-seed butter

Walnuts

Note: Limit quantities of nuts and seeds to a small handful at a time, and chew thoroughly.

Oils (cold-pressed only)

Almond oil (can be used for cooking)

Avocado oil (can be used for cooking)

Coconut oil (can be used for cooking)

Flaxseed oil (not for cooking)

Grapeseed oil (can be used for cooking)

*Oats do not contain gluten; however, they are sometimes cross-contaminated with other gluten grains. Therefore, when eating oats, purchase a brand that ensures that it is gluten-free, such as Bob's Red Mill.

Hempseed oil (not for cooking)

Olive oil (can be used for cooking, low heat only)

Pistachio oil (not for cooking; after 3 months)

Red palm fruit oil (can be used for cooking, low heat only)

Sesame oil (can be used for cooking)

Safflower oil (can be used for cooking)

Sunflower oil (can be used for cooking)

Walnut oil (not for cooking)

Note: At restaurants, eat what is served; be more stringent when using oils at home.

Dairy (antibiotic- and hormone-free only)

Butter (small amounts, unsalted, preferably organic from grass-fed cows)

Clarified butter (ghee, organic)

Goat cheese (raw;* small amounts after 3 months)

Sheep cheese (raw;* small amounts after 3 months)

Fruits† (organic; no dried fruit or fruit juices)

Apples (only sour green apples for first 3 months)

Avocado‡

Blackberries (discard if you see any visible mold)

Blueberries (discard if you see any visible mold)

Coconut flesh and/or unsweetened milk (no coconut juice or coconut water)

Cranberries (fresh, unsweetened)

Grapefruit

Lemons, limes‡

Olives (without vinegar or preservatives only)‡

Raspberries (discard if you see any visible mold)

Strawberries (discard if you see any visible mold)

Condiments

Apple cider vinegar (raw, unfiltered only—refrigerate)

Bragg Liquid Aminos (unfermented soy sauce; only acceptable soy product)

Dill relish (made without vinegar only; Bubbies; after 3 months)

Dry mustard (or small amounts of mustard made with apple cider vinegar)

Fresh herbs (basil, parsley, etc.)

Himalayan salt

Kelp flakes (Bragg Organic Sea Kelp Delight Seasoning)

Mayonnaise (see Recipes)

Pepper

Rice vinegar (unseasoned and unsweetened only—refrigerate)

Sea salt

Spices (without sugar, MSG, or additives); favor ginger and turmeric (anti-inflammatory)

Beverages

Bragg Apple Cider Vinegar Drinks (Ginger Spice, Limeade, and Sweet Stevia only)

Herbal teas (red clover, peppermint, green, etc.)

Suja Lemon Love (lemon juice drink)

Unsweetened almond, coconut, and hemp milk

Unsweetened mineral water (Gerolsteiner)

Water (filtered, purified, or distilled only)

Sweeteners

Chicory root (Just Like Sugar)

Lo han (luo han)

Stevia (Kal liquid)

Xylitol (small amounts; The Ultimate Sweetener, Xyla)

Miscellaneous

Cacao powder (raw, unsweetened; small amounts after 2 months)

Carob (unsweetened; small amounts after 2 months because it is an inflammatory legume)

Cocoa powder (unsweetened; small amounts after 2 months)

Coconut butter (organic)

Dill pickles (made without vinegar only; Bubbies; after 3 months)

Gums/mints (sweetened with lo han, stevia, or xylitol)

Salsa (without sugar or vinegar, except apple cider vinegar)

Sauerkraut (made without vinegar only; Bubbies; after 3 months)

---

*Pregnant and nursing women should not eat raw dairy products.

†Limit fruit intake to one piece per day, about the size of a medium apple in volume, or a handful of berries.

‡Avocado serving, lemon or lime juice, and olives may be in addition to your one fruit per day.

Foods to Avoid

Avoid the foods on this list while you are on the candida-cure diet. After three months (unless a different time period is specified), you may include the foods below marked with an asterisk (*). Add one food at a time every third day and see if your body reacts—i.e., rapid heartbeat, itching, bloating and gas, constipation, fatigue, or worsening of your symptoms. If this happens, keep these foods out of your diet for another three months and then try again if you wish.

Animal Protein

Bacon (except turkey bacon without nitrates and hormones; gluten-free)

Hotdogs (except chicken and turkey hotdogs without nitrates and hormones; gluten-free; small amounts because high in sodium)

Pork

Processed and packaged meats

Sausages (except chicken and turkey sausages that are gluten-, hormone-, antibiotic-, and nitrate-free)

Tuna (all: toro, albacore, ahi, etc., including canned)

Grains

Barley

Breads (except gluten-, dairy-, yeast-, and sugar-free, but not containing the grains listed here)

Cereals (except gluten-, dairy-, and sugar-free)

Corn (tortillas, polenta, popcorn, chips, etc.)

Crackers (except gluten-, dairy-, yeast-, and sugar-free; do not eat any with corn, potato, and/or white flour)

Farro

Kamut

Oats* (use gluten-free after 2 months)

Pasta (except those made from brown rice, buckwheat, quinoa)

Pastries

Rye

Spelt

Triticale

White flours

White rice

Wheat (refined)

Whole wheat

Vegetables

Corn

Mushrooms

Peas*

Potatoes

Beans and Legumes

You may eat small amounts once or twice a week or avoid these entirely for the first 2 months of the program because of their potential to cause inflammation and their high starch levels, which raise blood sugar. If you avoid them and then reintroduce, eat small amounts once or twice a week only, but continue to stay off soy (tofu, soybeans, tamari, and ponzu sauce), fermented soy products (miso, tempeh, etc.), and peas.

Nuts and Seeds

Cashews*

Peanuts, peanut butter

Pistachios*

Oils

Canola oil

Corn oil

Cottonseed oil

Peanut oil

Pistachio oil*

Processed oils and partially hydrogenated and hydrogenated oils

Soy oil

Dairy

Cheeses (all, including cottage and cream cheese)

Buttermilk

Cow's milk

Goat's milk and cheese* (raw okay after 3 months, small amounts)

Ice cream

Margarine

Sheep cheese* (raw okay after 3 months, small amounts)

Sour cream

Yogurt

Note: Pregnant and nursing women should not eat raw dairy products.

Fruits

Apricots*

Bananas*

Cherries*

Cranberries (sweetened)

Dried fruits (all, including apricots, dates, figs, raisins, cranberries, prunes, etc.)

Guavas*

Grapes*

Juices (all, sweetened or unsweetened)

Kiwis*

Mangoes*

Melons*

Nectarines*

Oranges*

Papayas*

Peaches*

Pears*

Pineapples*

Plums*

Persimmons*

Pomegranates*

Tangerines*

Beverages

Alcohol

Caffeinated teas (except green tea)†

Coffee (caffeinated and decaffeinated)

Energy drinks (e.g., Red Bull, vitamin waters)

Fruit juices

Kefir

Kombucha

Sodas (diet and regular)

Rice and soy milks

Condiments

Gravy

Jams and jellies

Ketchup (see Recipes)

Mayonnaise (see Recipes)

Mustard (unless made with apple cider vinegar; small amounts)

Pickles

Relish

Salad dressing (unless sugar-free and made with apple cider vinegar or unsweetened rice vinegar)

Sauces with vinegars and sugar

Soy sauce, ponzu, and tamari sauce

Spices that contain yeast, sugar, or additives

Vinegars (all, except raw, unfiltered apple cider vinegar and unsweetened rice vinegar—keep refrigerated)

Worcestershire sauce

Sweeteners

Agave nectar (Nectevia)

Artificial sweeteners, such as aspartame (Nutrasweet), acesulfame K, saccharin, and sucralose (Splenda)

Barley malt

Brown rice syrup

Brown sugar

Coconut sugar/nectar

Corn syrup

Dextrose

Erythritol (Nectresse, Swerve, Truvia)

Fructose, products sweetened with fruit juice

Honey (raw or processed; raw honey may be used medicinally)

Maltitol

Mannitol

Maltodextrin

Maple syrup

Molasses

Raw or evaporated cane juice crystals

Sorbitol

White sugar

Yacon syrup

Miscellaneous

Cacao/chocolate* (unless sweetened with stevia or xylitol; small amounts after 2 months)

Candy

Carob* (unsweetened, small amounts after 2 months because it is an inflammatory legume)

Cookies

Donuts

Fast food and fried foods

Fermented foods* (kimchi, sauerkraut, tempeh, yogurt, nutritional yeast, cultured vegetables, etc.)

Fruit strips

Gelatin

Gum (unless sweetened with stevia or xylitol)

Jerky (beef, turkey)

Lozenges/mints (unless sweetened with lo han, stevia, or xylitol)

Muffins

Pastries

Pizza

Processed food (TV dinners, etc.)

Smoked, dried, pickled, and cured foods

---

†Most people do best staying off all caffeine for the first 3 months on an anti-candida program. For those with autoimmune conditions or cancer, I recommend no caffeine during the first 2–3 months.

Making Healthy Choices

....

WHEN SEEKING TO EAT a healthy diet, there are some basic choices you can make to ensure you stay on the right track. The following information will give you some guidelines for creating meals that will support your body's work of rejuvenating itself.

Vegetables

If you want to stay healthy, eat a rainbow every day, as the saying goes. The more colors and variety of organic vegetables that you eat, the more phytonutrients you will take in. Experiment with different ways to prepare vegetables: raw, steamed, sautéed, baked, or in soups and stews. Or you can put them in a Vitamix, a juicer, or a NutriBullet and drink them. Aim to have vegetables make up 60 percent of your daily diet.

The most important vegetables to consume on a daily basis are dark leafy greens, such as spinach, watercress, collards, chard, broccoli, kale, arugula, and other dark-green lettuces. If you have a hypothyroid condition, you would do best to avoid eating large amounts of raw goitrogenic vegetables, such as kale, cauliflower, Brussels sprouts, spinach, and collards. Goitrogens are naturally occurring substances found in various foods that can disrupt thyroid function by interfering with iodine metabolism. Instead, cook these vegetables, which destroys most of their goitrogenic effects, or eat them raw in limited quantities.

Some people do not digest raw vegetables well, at least not until they correct some underlying physical imbalances. This is usually due to hypofunction of the pancreas, which results in low enzyme production, making food indigestible and difficult to absorb. Incomplete digestion can, in turn, cause an inflamed, leaky gut. It is best for these people to initially eat vegetables that are steamed, sautéed, baked, etc. Once candida levels are balanced, pancreas function is improved, and blood-sugar levels are stabilized, adding raw foods back into the diet is usually not a problem.

Avoid canned vegetables as much as possible. You will see that some of the recipes call for canned items, but these small amounts won't hurt you.

Grains

Gluten is a protein composite of gliadin and glutenin, found in wheat, barley, rye, triticale, kamut, spelt, oats (by cross-contamination in factories that make wheat), and white flour. Everyone today can benefit from living gluten-free, since gluten is attributed to inflammation and leaky gut in the body.

Gluten-free grains and flours, except for corn, are allowed in small quantities on the candida program. They include amaranth, brown rice, gluten-free oats, sorghum, and teff. Gluten-free seeds and flours include buckwheat, kañiwa, quinoa, and millet. Though often referred to as grains, these are actually seeds. Even though corn is gluten-free, it is high in carbohydrates, and in the United States 90 percent of it is genetically modified. Therefore it is not allowed on an anti-candida diet.

Soaking grains makes them more digestible by eliminating most of their phytic acid, which interferes with mineral absorption. Thirty minutes to one hour of soaking and rinsing is sufficient, and good to do if you have the time. However, if, like many, you are challenged with a hectic schedule, soaking is not a must, but at least rinse grains to remove any dirt, mold, etc.

Grains contain important B vitamins, which help keep your nervous system in balance. They also have fiber to help you eliminate daily and keep your colon lining healthy. The problem is that most people eat too much from this food group, when only 25 to 50 grams of carbohydrates a day are needed by the body. I recommend living gluten-free and corn-free even after completing your candida program since these substances can aggravate the body.

Note: Some people might heal faster by staying off grains for one to three months until their gastrointestinal tracts and blood-sugar levels are balanced. If you have an autoimmune condition or chronic gastrointestinal issue, it might be worth experimenting to see how you do. However, for some, this may result in too much weight loss and fatigue.

Herbs and Spices

Adding culinary herbs and spices to recipes is one of the easiest and most inexpensive ways to heal the body. Herbs and spices are packed with nutrient-rich properties. Rosemary is an antioxidant and stimulates circulation. Turmeric is anti-inflammatory. Cilantro and parsley are excellent heavy-metal chelators and free-radical scavengers. Oregano and thyme are powerful antimicrobials, and cinnamon helps balance blood sugar. The list goes on and on. Use them! Don't be afraid to experiment or ad lib with the recipes.

Make sure to read ingredient labels on dried spices to make sure that they do not have added sugar, oils, MSG, or nutritional yeast.

Sea Vegetables

Integrating these foods from the sea into your diet will provide you with an excellent source of natural iodine. Deficiency of this mineral can contribute to various thyroid conditions, which are prevalent among so many people today. Iodine is not only essential for a healthy thyroid, but also for healthy breast tissue, ovaries, and prostates. Arame, dulse, nori, hijiki, kelp, kombu, and wakame are common sea vegetables that you can use in your recipes, nibble on as a snack, or sprinkle on your food. Sheets of nori can also be used to make seafood or veggie rolls.

Nuts and Seeds

Organic raw nuts and seeds are high in the good fats that your body needs. Flaxseeds and chia seeds are an excellent source of fiber, which supports healthy elimination and keeps cholesterol levels balanced. On the downside, eating too many nuts and seeds can congest the gallbladder, make you constipated, or cause skin breakouts. Certain nuts are also high in carbohydrates, which will feed candida. So the key is to eat only small handfuls of nuts and seeds at a time and to chew them thoroughly so that you digest them more easily. Refrigerate nuts and seeds in mason jars after opening to keep them from going rancid. Toasting them in the oven or in a skillet over low heat are great ways to make your own yummy dry-roasted nuts and seeds. Soaking makes certain nuts and seeds more digestible—though this is just an option, not a must.

Animal Protein

Your healthiest options are organic, pasture-raised, and antibiotic- and hormone-free meats and eggs. Look for the words *pastured* or *pasture-raised* on meat packages and egg cartons. That means the animals have been allowed to roam freely outdoors and eat natural forage. Labels that say "cage-free" or "free-range" do not necessarily mean the animals have received this kind of treatment, or that they have been treated humanely. Depending on where you live, your options may be limited, so just be mindful and do the best you can with what is available in your town or country.

The amount of animal protein each person needs varies based on an individual's weight, gender, and blood-sugar levels. I recommend one to two servings daily of two to four ounces per meal. For most people, that is sufficient to help the body heal and stabilize. I have found that those who prefer less animal protein do best eating no less than three servings a week and taking a vitamin B12 and a free-form amino acid supplement. Those with hypoglycemia do well eating animal protein twice daily, especially at breakfast to help keep energy levels stable throughout the day. If you eat red meat (beef, bison, lamb, buffalo), I suggest having it no more than once a week to reduce potential problems with digestion, acidity, and saturated fat. Combine red meat with green vegetables only (no starchy vegetables, beans, or grains) to make it easier to digest and less acidic.

Fish are becoming more and more contaminated with heavy metals due to industrial pollution and radiation from nuclear accidents. Fish highly contaminated with mercury include all forms of tuna (canned, fresh, and as sushi), tilapia, mackerel, swordfish, tilefish, shark, and orange roughy. I suggest avoiding them as well as farmed fish, which are raised with antibiotics and colored with dye. Atlantic salmon, cod, sole, and halibut are usually farmed. Eat only small amounts of wild-caught shellfish, as many are contaminated from oil spills and other pollutants.

Beans and Legumes

Beans and legumes are a good source of fiber, vitamins, minerals, and amino acids. Make sure to buy organic and soak beans overnight (time permitting) to help break down the phytic acid, which can block mineral absorption. If you are following a candida program, eat only small amounts once or twice a week, as beans and legumes are high in starch, which converts to sugar in the body and, in turn, will feed the yeast. Mung beans and adzuki beans are higher in protein than other beans and are therefore a good choice when on an anti-candida diet.

People with autoimmune conditions who are following a candida program should avoid beans and legumes for the first three months or longer since they can cause inflammation.

Soy is commonly genetically modified in the United States and therefore to be avoided as much as possible. Though fermented organic soy is better for you than processed and GM soy, it is not allowed on an anti-candida diet. I have found that people who are not sensitive to soy do okay using small amounts of Bragg Liquid Aminos, which is an unfermented form of soy sauce. However, those who are sensitive may react because there is naturally occurring MSG in soy.

Good Fats

Good fats, such as omega 3, 6, and 9, are needed for the integrity of every cell membrane and are important for brain, skin, and heart health as well as hormonal balance. Foods such as avocados, coconuts, fish, nuts, seeds, unsalted grass-fed butter, and many oils contain these good fats. Some oils cannot be heated because they will become rancid. You can find charts and information on the Internet that give the smoke points for different oils. These are the temperatures at which the oil decomposes and becomes unhealthy to consume. Oils that cannot be heated are great to drizzle on salads or vegetables, make into a dressing, or lightly pour over an entrée. Avocado and coconut oils are good substitutes for safflower and grapeseed oils and can be used for high-heat cooking.

Sweeteners

Four sweeteners are allowed on an anti-candida diet: (1) stevia, (2) xylitol, preferably from a birch source; a non-GMO corn source would be the second option, (3) lo han, also known as monk fruit, and (4) chicory root; Just Like Sugar is a common brand. Some brands of xylitol are coarse, so you can use a food processor or coffee grinder to refine it. Xylitol is a sugar alcohol and the only one in this category that I recommend because this substance is naturally manufactured in small amounts in our bodies during carbohydrate metabolism. Even though it is a carbohydrate, eating it in small quantities is okay since it is metabolized slowly and therefore does not increase sugar levels rapidly.

Be aware that sugar alcohols, including xylitol, can aggravate your digestive system if consumed in large quantities, causing gas, bloating, pain, or diarrhea. Large quantities will also feed candida because of the carbohydrate content. Typically, one to two teaspoons of xylitol a day will not feed candida, though I prefer that you eat desserts containing it only two to three times a week.

If you are sensitive to xylitol, you may substitute stevia, lo han, or chicory root (see suggested conversions on page 32). Since stevia can significantly change the taste of a recipe, it may not always work well as a substitute. You will need to experiment by adjusting the ratios to suit your taste when using it as a substitute for xylitol.

Fruits

Limiting fruits while on an anti-candida diet is necessary because even though they contain natural sugar, too much sugar in any form will feed yeast and fungus. On my "Foods to Eat" list, I recommend eating only one fruit per day. In addition to this, you may have avocados, lemons, limes, and olives (not prepared in vinegar brine) since the sugars in these fruits are low.

Flours

Gluten- and grain-free flours are used in the recipes in this book. You can now choose from a wide array of these types of flours to bake and cook with. Coconut, almond, and Brazil nut flours are among my personal favorites.

Fiber

Soluble and insoluble fiber are essential for a healthy gastrointestinal system and regular elimination. Flaxseeds, hempseeds, and chia seeds are excellent sources and are high in omega 3 fatty acids. Raw vegetables are also one of the best sources of fiber.

Fermented Foods and Nutritional Yeast

I recommend staying off all fermented foods, such as sauerkraut, kefir, cultured vegetables, kimchi, kombucha, tempeh, yogurt, etc., when following an anti-candida diet. While these do not directly feed candida in the same way that sugar does, fermented foods are high in histamines and can initially aggravate a body that has candida overgrowth. Also avoid nutritional yeast and brewer's yeast because those with candida tend to have an allergic reaction to them. It's important to wait until your gut ecology is more balanced, preferably after sixty to ninety days of being on an anti-candida diet, before eating any fermented or yeast-based foods. When you do introduce them, start slowly and see if they agree with your body.

The exceptions in this category are raw apple cider vinegar, which has many beneficial properties for overall health; unsweetened rice vinegar; and Raw Coconut Aminos, made by Coconut Secret. I have found that these products do not interfere with people's progress on a candida program.

Beverages

It's important to stay hydrated by drinking six ounces of purified water each waking hour. Many people do not like the taste of water. One way to get around that and improve the taste is to put a teabag of your favorite herbal tea in your water container. Both hot and cold teas count as water, but be sure to also drink water since most teas act as diuretics. Drinking tea is an inexpensive way to keep the body healthy. Red clover, dandelion root, hibiscus, chamomile, mint, yew, other herbal teas, and green tea have healing properties. When purchasing prepared teas, make sure that there are no added sweeteners or dried fruits in them.

You will find that almond milk is called for in several of the recipes. You may substitute any unsweetened nondairy milk, such as hemp or coconut, but do not use soy or rice milks.

The Importance of Buying Organic and Local

....

TODAY OUR FOOD SUPPLY is under attack from the use of hormones, antibiotics, herbicides, pesticides, and fungicides. These chemicals create inflammation and disrupt optimal cellular function in the body. I cannot stress enough the importance of buying organic, pasture-raised, grass-fed, and antibiotic- and hormone-free foods. If you do not have access to or cannot afford organic vegetables, fruits, meats, eggs, nuts, etc., do your best. Buy as much fresh produce as you can. The next best thing is frozen foods, but use as few canned foods as possible.

If you have to buy conventional vegetables and fruits, purchase those with thick skins, such as avocados, grapefruit, and pineapple, rather than fruits and vegetables like broccoli, celery, and strawberries, whose surfaces are directly exposed to toxins.

Support local vendors by buying their products from your health food stores and farmers' markets. Not only will the food be fresher and more nutritious, but buying local supports your community and eliminates long-distance transport, helping to reduce fuel emissions. If possible, start your own small organic herb and vegetable garden. Nothing tastes better than eating your own homegrown herbs and vegetables.

When you can't buy local or find any of the items listed in the recipes, you may be able to purchase them online. The best discount online sources are amazon.com, iherb.com, thrivemarket .com, and vitacost.com.

Tips and Substitutions

....

THE FOLLOWING TIPS and guidelines for purchasing and preparation will help you successfully create the recipes in this book and tailor them to your own needs. I suggest that you read these guidelines carefully and refer back to them whenever necessary.

Buying Packaged Foods

The ingredients listed below are called for in many of the recipes. When purchasing, make sure they meet the following criteria:

- **Baking powder and baking soda:** aluminum-free
- **Broths (vegetable or chicken):** organic and unsweetened
- **Butter:** unsalted, organic, from grass-fed cows (pasture-raised)
- **Canned ingredients:** for ingredients such as beans, coconut milk, and tomato sauce that come in cans, buy those that are organic with no added sweeteners
- **Capers:** prepared without vinegar
- **Cocoa powder:** unsweetened only
- **Extracts such as vanilla, mint, and lemon:** alcohol- and sugar-free. If you cannot find these in a local store, you can purchase them online. If for some reason you must use extracts containing alcohol, know that much of the alcohol will evaporate when it is heated.
- **Hot sauces:** preservative-free and vinegar-free only (except if made with apple cider vinegar)
- **Mustard:** made with apple cider vinegar only, not white vinegar
- **Olive oil:** extra-virgin, organic
- **Olives:** prepared without vinegar brine
- **Shredded coconut:** organic and unsweetened
- **Sun-dried tomatoes packed in olive oil:** sulfite-free only

Soaking Grains, Seeds, Nuts, and Beans

- Soaking is not essential, but is an option for those who have the time to do it.
- When soaking, always use purified or filtered water, adding enough to cover beans, nuts, seeds, or grains by at least two inches. Drain and rinse well before using. If not using them right away, make sure to store in the refrigerator to prevent mold growth, and consume them within 1–3 days.

- Recommended soaking times:

  Grains: 30 minutes –1 hour

  Seeds (sunflower, pumpkin, sesame, etc.): 4–8 hours

  Nuts: Soaking times usually range from 4–8 hours. The harder the nut, the longer it will need to soak. Make sure to store soaked nuts and seeds in the refrigerator to prevent mold growth, and consume them within 1–3 days.

  Beans: 4–6 hours or overnight if possible

- **Rinsing unsoaked seeds, nuts, grains, and beans:** It is a good idea to rinse these before using or cooking them because of the dust that they may have picked up in bulk bins and in production.
- When using soaked seeds or nuts in a recipe that calls for blending, pour off the soaking water and rinse the seeds or nuts before blending them with the other ingredients. If they're not soaked, just rinse and drain them before blending.

Washing and Peeling Produce

- Wash all vegetables and fruits in purified or distilled water (even if they are organic), using soap and water or a specially made fruit-and-vegetable wash, which you can find at your health food store or online. Or you can soak them in raw apple cider vinegar for about a half hour before eating. If you're in a hurry, give them a quick rinse, even if the package says they have been triple-washed.
- Wash produce on the day you will be eating or cooking it to prevent mold growth. Berries, especially, get moldy quickly (eating moldy food will aggravate candida).
- When washing greens, dry before adding to salads.
- Wash thick-skinned vegetables, such as acorn squash, before baking.
- When using organic root vegetables, such as beets, turnips, and sweet potatoes, you do not need to peel them, as there are a lot of nutrients in and right under the skin. Cut off the tough ends of certain root vegetables, such as rutabaga and turnips, and scrub well in soapy water with a vegetable brush. Peel conventional, nonorganic root vegetables since pesticides concentrate in the skin.

More Prep Tips

- **Chiffonade:** When this cut is called for (usually for basil), stack the leaves, tightly roll them up like a burrito, and thinly slice crosswise.
- **Coconut cream:** Coconut cream is generally firm but may get runny if the temperature is warm. When using it for a recipe that specifies that cream should be firm, place the can in the refrigerator for 1–2 hours to firm it up. Be sure to use coconut cream, and not coconut milk, when cream is called for in a recipe.
- **Coconut milk:** Full-fat coconut milk may sometimes be solid but will liquefy if you add it to hot foods.

- **Coconut oil:** Coconut oil has a melting point of 76 degrees Fahrenheit, so it will be solid unless your kitchen is below that temperature. When a recipe requires the oil to be liquefied, you can either place the jar in a bowl of hot water or gently heat the oil in a small saucepan over low heat.
- **Greasing pans:** Many recipes call for coconut or olive oil spray to grease baking pans, which is a convenient option. If you do not have these sprays, you may simply apply the regular form of the oil by spreading it evenly on the pan with a paper towel or a brush. (Also see "Silicone cookware" below.)
- **Onion sliced in half moons:** When a recipe calls for this cut, peel the onion and cut off the ends. Cut onion in half lengthwise (along the onion ribs) and slice into half moons to desired thickness.
- **Quinoa:** Before soaking or cooking, rinse quinoa under cold running water in a fine-mesh strainer to remove both the dirt and its natural coating, which tastes bitter. A regular-sized strainer will allow the tiny quinoa seeds to slip through. After quinoa has cooked for the required amount of time, remove the pan from the burner and keep the lid on for another 5 minutes to prevent quinoa from sticking to the bottom of the pan.
- **Toasting seeds:** Some recipes call for sunflower, pumpkin, or sesame seeds to be toasted. To toast, place them in a small skillet over low heat and stir continuously for about 3–5 minutes. Be careful, as seeds will burn quickly if not constantly moving. Remove from burner when the seeds begin to release their aroma. You can also toast them in the oven: preheat to 325°F, spread seeds on a baking sheet, and bake until they release their aroma, around 10–15 minutes. These techniques can also be used for toasting nuts.
- **Zesting and juicing citrus:** When a recipe calls for the zest of a lemon, lime, or orange, wash the fruit well with soap and water and grate only the surface layer of the peel, taking care not to grate into the white rind, which is bitter. When juicing lemons and limes, you may do this by hand or with a lemon squeezer or citrus juicer. To loosen the juice, roll them on the counter with your palm before squeezing.

Tools
- **Box grater:** Use for shredding, grating, and shaving vegetables.
- **Parchment paper:** Use unbleached, which is better for your health.
- **Silicone cookware:** Even though silicone cookware—including muffin/cupcake tins and egg poachers—help prevent sticking, to be effective they still need to be sprayed or otherwise coated with coconut or olive oil, as instructed in the recipes.
- **Spiralizer:** This is a great tool for making vegetable "noodles."
- **Vitamix or high-speed blender:** A high-powered blender allows you to thoroughly blend raw vegetables and fruits in smoothies and sauces. The Vitamix is also great for blending soups. A NutriBullet is a small-sized blender that can be used for making smoothies.

To Save Time
- Many of the recipes can be made in quantity and either stored in the refrigerator for up to 3 days or in the freezer for up to 3 months.
- Make a couple of batches of Brazil Nut Parmesan "Cheese" and Herbed Sunflower Spread in advance and store in small containers in the freezer (for up to 3 months). This will eliminate an extra step when they are called for in recipes.
- When making Garlic-Rosemary Paleo Bread (with or without olives), place 3 to 4 slices in individual containers and freeze (for up to 2 months).

Health and Safety First
- When working with jalapeño peppers, wear rubber gloves when seeding so that you do not burn your hands or eyes by accidentally rubbing them after you have finished preparing the peppers.
- When adding hot or boiled liquids to a blender, place a dish towel over the lid to protect your hand. Fill the blender only half to three-quarters full so it doesn't overflow when blending. Start blending at a low speed, and gradually bring the blender up to the higher speed required. You may have to blend in more than one batch.
- When mixing hot foods, use glass, ceramic, or stainless steel bowls. Do not use plastic, as this can cause melting and/or the leaching of toxic chemicals from the plastic into the food.
- **Nonstick skillets:** I recommend using ceramic-coated stainless steel skillets. Use wooden or nonmetal utensils with these so that you do not damage the cookware's surface.
- Rinse meat, poultry, and fish under cold running water before preparing, being careful not to get rinsing water on anything in the sink, such as cutting boards, utensils, or dishes.

Miscellaneous Essentials
- **Baking:** Baking times may vary depending on your oven and where you live. Higher altitudes usually require longer cooking times, so adjust your timing accordingly.
- **Refrigeration and storage:** It is best to refrigerate flours, nuts, and seeds, preferably in mason jars, to keep them fresh and prevent them from getting rancid. Also refrigerate any leftovers of any of the recipes.
- **Water:** When water is called for in any recipe, always use purified or filtered water, not tap water, which may contain fluoride, chlorine, microorganisms, and other toxic substances.

Substitutions

- **Raw Coconut Aminos:** When a recipe calls for Raw Coconut Aminos, you may replace it with sea salt, using the following conversion formula: 1 tablespoon of Raw Coconut Aminos = ¼ teaspoon sea salt.
- **Xylitol substitutes:** Xylitol can be replaced with stevia, chicory root (Just Like Sugar—Table Top), or lo han. Ratios will vary, depending on the recipe (see below).
- **Xylitol/stevia ratios:** Stevia is very sweet, so when substituting it for xylitol, you will use much less of it. (Some brands of stevia are sweeter than others and leave an aftertaste. I recommend using Kal Pure Stevia liquid, as it tastes the best and has little or no aftertaste.) The recipes often suggest a range in the amount of stevia to use. The equivalencies I have listed in the chart below and throughout the recipes for replacing xylitol with stevia are approximate. Experiment and adjust the amounts to your taste, initially starting on the low end to be safe. (Also note that if buying stevia powder, make sure it is pure and does not contain any fillers or additives, which are sometimes corn-based. Those forms of stevia will be much less potent, and therefore these conversion ratios will not apply.)

Xylitol	Stevia liquid	Stevia powder
1 cup	1 teaspoon	1 teaspoon
1 tablespoon	5–6 drops	¼ teaspoon
1 teaspoon	2 drops	1 pinch–$\frac{1}{16}$ teaspoon

- **Xylitol/chicory and xylitol/lo han ratios:** When substituting chicory root (Just Like Sugar, for example) or lo han for xylitol, use an even one-to-one ratio.

Suggested Brands

. . . .

Stocking your kitchen with many of the brands listed below will make it easier to create the recipes at a moment's notice. If you live outside the U.S. and cannot obtain these brands, you can order them from online websites such as amazon.com, iherb.com, thrivemarket.com, or vitacost.com.

Apple cider vinegar, raw	Bragg, Spectrum
Arrowroot starch/flour	Bob's Red Mill
Baking powder and baking soda	Bob's Red Mill (aluminum-free)
Beverages and teas	Yerba Maté Royale (Wisdom of the Ancients) Traditional Medicinals, Bragg Organic Apple Cider Vinegar Drinks (only stevia-sweetened ones)
Butter (organic, unsalted, from grass-fed cows)	Kerrygold Pure Irish Butter, Straus European Style
Chicory root	Just Like Sugar—Table Top
Coconut cream and milk (organic if possible, canned or in cartons)	Thai Kitchen, Native Forest, Trader Joe's, So Delicious, Trader Joe's Coconut Cream: Extra Thick & Rich
Curry paste	Thai Kitchen Red Curry Paste
Dried herbs and spices	The Spice Hunter, Simply Organic
Flour, gluten-free: tapioca, coconut, almond meal/flour	Bob's Red Mill
Gluten-free noodles	Annie Chun's Brown Rice Noodles
Hot sauces	Arizona Pepper's Organic Harvest Foods, Brother Bru Bru's
Mustard	Eden Foods
Oils	Spectrum
Raw Coconut Aminos	Coconut Secret
Refried beans	Trader Joe's Refried Black Beans with Jalapeño Peppers, Amy's Vegetarian Organic Refried Black Beans
Stevia	Kal Pure Stevia Extract (liquid), SweetLeaf Stevia powder
Tomato sauce	Muir Glen Organic
Vegetable broth (in cartons)	Trader Joe's, Whole Foods
Xylitol	Xyla USA, Ultimate Life

Pantry Stock List

....

BUY ORGANIC WHENEVER POSSIBLE. Though this list is lengthy, your initial investment will provide you with items that will last for months. Many of these products can be purchased from online discount websites such as amazon.com, iherb.com, thrivemarket.com, and vitacost.com, which can save you time and money.

Dried Herbs and Spices
Allspice
Black pepper
Cardamom, ground
Cayenne pepper
Chili powder
Chinese 5 spice
Cinnamon, ground
Cloves, ground
Coriander, ground
Cumin, whole and ground
Curry powder
Garlic powder
Ginger, ground
Italian herbs
Nutmeg, ground
Oregano
Red pepper flakes
Rosemary
Sage
Sea salt or Himalayan salt
Smoked paprika
Star anise
Thyme
Turmeric, ground

Note: Store spices in a cool place, not over the stove or in a hot area, to extend their life.

Nuts and Seeds (raw)
Almonds, slivered and whole
Brazil nuts
Pecans
Pumpkin seeds
Sesame seeds
Sunflower seeds
Walnuts

Milks
Almond, unsweetened
Coconut, unsweetened
Hempseed, unsweetened

Broths
Organic chicken broth, in cartons, unsweetened
Organic vegetable broth, in cartons, unsweetened

Flours/Leavening Agents/ Binders
Almond meal and flour
Arrowroot starch/flour
Baking powder, aluminum-free
Baking soda, aluminum-free
Brown rice flour
Coconut flour
Sorghum flour
Tapioca starch
Teff flour

Dry Cereals
Amaranth
Buckwheat groats
Oats, gluten-free
Quinoa flakes
Teff

Sweeteners
Chicory root
Stevia liquid or powder
Xylitol

Oils
Avocado oil
Coconut oil
Grapeseed oil
Olive oil, extra virgin
Safflower oil

Miscellaneous
Coconut, shredded unsweetened
Coconut oil spray
Olive oil spray
Pumpkin puree, canned, organic, unsweetened
Raw Coconut Aminos

Extracts (preferably alcohol-free)
Almond
Coconut
Lemon
Vanilla

Equipment and Tools

·························

STOCKING UP YOUR KITCHEN with gadgets and equipment will make for an easier food preparation experience. Not everything on the list is mandatory—get what you can.

Blender (Vitamix or less expensive high-powered blender)

Baking sheets

Box grater

Bread loaf pan

Crock Pot slow cooker

Fine-mesh strainer

Food processor

Juicer (Breville preferred)

Knives, sharp

Measuring spoons and cups

Meat thermometer

Microplane to zest lemons and limes

Nut milk bag

Oil brush

Parchment paper, unbleached

Pie dish

Plastic gloves

Quart pans

Sifter

Silicone muffin/cupcake tins or cups

Slotted spoon

Spiralizer

Stockpot

Skillets (stainless steel or ceramic-coated; stay away from aluminum and limit use of cast iron)

Waffle iron

Whisk

Wooden spoons

Four-Week Menu Plan

....

SOME PEOPLE WHO ARE just starting out on a candida program get stuck because they don't know what to eat at each meal or cannot conceptualize what a week of eating would look like. The four-week menu plan that follows is designed to give you some ideas for the many delicious meals you can create while on a candida program, which will help you stick to the diet. You will find recipes for the starred (*) dishes in the recipes section of this book.

Eating snacks is optional. Be aware that if you want to lose weight, eating snacks will speed up your metabolism. If you don't want to lose weight, you will do better eating only three meals a day, with no snacks, as this will slow down your metabolism. In either case, the most important thing to remember is not to skip meals. Doing so disrupts your blood-sugar levels and creates hypoglycemia, which can make you feel jittery, irritable, weak, and spacey as well as cause headaches and increase cravings for sugar, carbs, and caffeine.

Note: If you would like to add something more to a dish in order to feel satisfied and full, consider adding a piece of animal protein, such as grilled fish, baked chicken, or a turkey breast. Those who are hypoglycemic (have low blood sugar) should make sure to have some form of protein at breakfast (eggs, chicken, turkey, fish, protein powder, etc.) for the first month of the program or longer, until blood-sugar levels are balanced.

Week 1

DAY 1

Breakfast	Broccoli and Yellow-Onion Egg Muffins*
Snack	Spinach and Artichoke Dip* with sliced raw vegetables (cucumber, jicama, broccoli)
Lunch	Caesar Chicken Salad*
Snack	Handful of Savory Nut Mix*
Dinner	Vegan Grain-Free Lasagna*
	Cucumber-Avocado Salad*

DAY 2

Breakfast	Blueberry-Coconut Quinoa Porridge* with a side of chicken sausage
Snack	Vegetable Alkalizer Juice*
Lunch	Creamy Zucchini Noodle Salad*
Snack	Pesto* dip with sliced raw vegetables (carrots, asparagus, celery)
Dinner	Macadamia-Crusted Halibut*
	Purple Cabbage Vegetable Medley*

DAY 3

Breakfast	Poached Eggs and Turkey-Bacon Salad*
Snack	Half a grapefruit with minced mint
Lunch	Shredded Raw Rainbow Salad*
Snack	Toasted Garlic-Rosemary Paleo Bread* with ghee
Dinner	Stuffed Cornish Hen with Wild Rice*
	Mixed green salad with Italian dressing*

DAY 4

Breakfast	Creamy Cinnamon-Coconut Buckwheat Porridge*
Snack	Hard-boiled egg with mustard
Lunch	Spring Quinoa Salad*
Snack	Coconut Cream Parfait*
Dinner	Ginger Beef and Broccoli*

DAY 5

Breakfast   Sun-Dried Tomato and Asparagus Quiche*

Snack   Celery sticks with sunflower-seed butter

Lunch   Black Bean Quesadillas*

Snack   Vegetable Alkalizer Juice*

Dinner   Mexican-Style Turkey Meatloaf*

      Mixed baby greens salad with lemon and olive oil

DAY 6

Breakfast   Gluten-Free Coconut-Raspberry Pancakes* with Coconut "Syrup"*

Snack   Crispy Baked Kale Chips*

Lunch   Egg salad in lettuce wraps with a side of black or green olives

Snack   Spicy Guacamole* with sliced raw vegetables

Dinner   Hearty Chicken-Vegetable Soup*

      Garlic-Rosemary and Olive Paleo Bread* with organic pasture butter

DAY 7

Breakfast   Egg-white omelet with sautéed onions and Swiss chard

Snack   Handful of blueberries, raspberries, or boysenberries

Lunch   Roasted Butternut Squash and Marinated Red Onion Salad*

Snack   Ginger-Spiced Cookies* with cup of red clover tea or Dandelion-Ginger Twist*

Dinner   Chicken Salad* topped on avocado halves

Week 2

DAY 1

Breakfast   Diced chicken or turkey sausage with sautéed onions, fresh herbs, and spinach in a lettuce wrap

Snack   Sun-Dried Tomato and Walnut Pesto* with sliced raw vegetables

Lunch   Red Quinoa Taco Salad*

Snack   Lemon Bars*

Dinner   Baked Cod with Olive Tapenade*

      Macadamia-Roasted Brussels Sprouts*

DAY 2

Breakfast	Pumpkin Granola* with Almond Milk* or Brazil Nut Milk*
Snack	Hibiscus Mint Tea* and sliced grapefruit
Lunch	Vegan Sunburger* in lettuce wrap
Snack	Arame with Carrots and Onions*
Dinner	Bison-Stuffed Bell Peppers*
	Watercress Salad*

DAY 3

Breakfast	Egg-white burrito: sautéed spinach, jalapeño (optional), tomato, and yellow onion with mashed avocado and Brazil Nut Parmesan "Cheese"* in a lettuce wrap or toasted Grain-Free Wrap*
Snack	Vegetable Alkalizer Juice*
Lunch	Almond Kale Salad*
Snack	Green apple with handful of raw walnuts
Dinner	Spiced Turkey Lettuce Wraps*

DAY 4

Breakfast	Almond Chai-Spiced Porridge*
Snack	Hot and Spicy Harissa* and sliced raw vegetables
Lunch	Turkey Chili with Sunflower "Sour Cream"*
Snack	Spicy Asian Coleslaw*
Dinner	Baked salmon with Olive Tapenade*
	Marinated Kale Salad*

DAY 5

Breakfast	Soft-boiled eggs with sautéed greens
Snack	Gluten-Free Zucchini Muffin*
Lunch	Baked Mac and "Cheese"* on a bed of leafy greens
Snack	Vegetable Alkalizer Juice*
Dinner	Roasted Garlic Chicken with Chimichurri* sauce
	Roasted Rosemary Vegetables*

DAY 6

Breakfast	Oatmeal Breakfast Bake* with a side of turkey bacon
Snack	Baked Kabocha Squash Slices*
Lunch	Chef's Salad*
Snack	Green Protein Power Smoothie*
Dinner	Eggplant Pizza with Brazil Nut Parmesan "Cheese"*
	Watercress Salad*

DAY 7

Breakfast	Lemon-Blueberry Waffles* with Fresh Berry "Syrup"*
Snack	Carrot-Walnut Pâte* with sliced raw vegetables
Lunch	Spicy Lime Chicken Taco with Cabbage Slaw*
	Mixed baby greens salad with Italian Dressing*
Snack	Leek and Onion Soup*
Dinner	Turkey Meatballs and Collards*

Week 3

DAY 1

Breakfast	Poached eggs over steamed kale or spinach, topped with Olive and Sun-Dried Tomato Tapenade*
Snack	Quick-and-Fresh Salsa* with flax crackers
Lunch	Oven-roasted sliced vegetable wrap (lettuce, Grain-Free Wrap,* or brown-rice tortilla) with Pesto* or Basil Herb Sauce*
Snack	Celery sticks with macadamia nut butter
Dinner	Kickin' Crab Cakes with Tartar Sauce*
	Spinach and Beet Salad*

DAY 2

Breakfast	Leek and Onion Quiche*
Snack	Nacho "Cheese" Dip* and sliced raw vegetables
Lunch	Tri-Color Quinoa Ginger-Mint Salad*
Snack	Cream of Asparagus Soup* with flax crackers
Dinner	Coconut Curry Vegetables* with chopped chicken breast

DAY 3

Breakfast	Mixed Vegetable Scramble* topped with sliced hard-boiled egg
Snack	Vegetable Alkalizer Juice*
Lunch	Thai-Spiced Kabocha Squash Soup*
Snack	Apple-Almond Butter Sandwiches*
Dinner	Seared Wild Salmon with Horseradish*
	Mixed baby greens salad with Hempseed Ranch Dip*

DAY 4

Breakfast	Pumpkin-Spiced Pancakes*
Snack	Carrot-Cumin Spread* with sliced raw vegetables
Lunch	Apple-Spiced Turkey Burgers* in a lettuce wrap
	Sweet Potato Fries*
Snack	Half a grapefruit sprinkled with ground cinnamon
Dinner	Quinoa Tabbouleh* and Tahini Sauce*
	Cucumber-Avocado Salad*

DAY 5

Breakfast	Egg-white omelet with diced vegetables, topped with Quick- and-Fresh Salsa*
Snack	Strawberries 'n' Cream Protein Smoothie*
Lunch	Spicy Buckwheat and Quinoa Stir-Fry*
Snack	Artichoke with Homemade Mayonnaise*
Dinner	Turkey-vegetable soup
	Garlic-Rosemary Paleo Bread* with ghee or pasture butter

DAY 6

Breakfast	Raspberry-Almond Amaranth and Teff Porridge* with a side of chicken sausage or turkey bacon
Snack	Green apple slices with sunflower-seed butter
Lunch	Herbed Vegetable Puree*
	Avocado, Hearts of Palm, and Pine Nut Salad*
Snack	Baked Berry Crumble* with cup of red clover tea or Hot Yerba Maté Latte*
Dinner	Macadamia-Crusted Trout*
	Cauliflower Thai Rice*
	Arugula salad with Italian Dressing*

DAY 7

Breakfast	Poached eggs with sautéed peppers, onions, and spinach, collards, or chard
Snack	Hummus* with sliced raw vegetables
Lunch	Salmon Salad*
Snack	Vegetable Nori Rolls*
Dinner	Spaghetti Squash Pasta with Spicy Lamb Red Sauce*

Week 4

DAY 1

Breakfast	Chicken Salad* in lettuce wraps
Snack	Sweet Nut Mix*
Lunch	Almond Kale Salad* with grilled turkey breast
Snack	Salsa Verde* with flax crackers
Dinner	Lemon-Lime Marinated Sole*
	Herbed Wild Rice Pilaf*

DAY 2

Breakfast	Green Protein Power Smoothie*
Snack	Guacamole* and gluten-free crackers
Lunch	Chicken-Vegetable Korma*
Snack	Watercress Salad*
	Lavender Lemonade*
Dinner	Pad Thai Noodles with Grilled Salmon* and garlic butter sauce
	Mixed baby greens salad with Tahini Sauce*

DAY 3

Breakfast	Spinach and Red Onion Frittata*
Snack	Vegetable Alkalizer Juice*
Lunch	Herbed Cauliflower Soup*
	Baked sweet potato with butter and chopped raw pecans
Snack	Quinoa Cakes*
Dinner	Macadamia-Crusted Mahi-Mahi*
	Lemon-Roasted Asparagus*

DAY 4

Breakfast   Grain-Free Wrap* with sautéed vegetables, sunny-side-up egg,
and Quick-and-Fresh Salsa*

Snack   Brown-rice cake with pumpkin butter

Lunch   Roasted Beef Bone Marrow Broth* with slice of toasted Garlic-Rosemary Paleo
Bread* and ghee or butter
Garden salad with Italian Dressing*

Snack   Hempseed Ranch Dip* with sliced raw vegetables

Dinner   Baked trout with thyme butter
Steamed Baby Bok Choy*

DAY 5

Breakfast   Pumpkin-Pie-Spiced Oatmeal* with a side of chicken sausage or
a chicken breast

Snack   Tender Collards and Onions*

Lunch   Roasted Rosemary Vegetables* with Pesto* on Garlic-Rosemary and
Olive Paleo Bread*

Snack   Coconut Muffins*

Dinner   Lamb Chili with Sunflower "Sour Cream"*
Mixed greens salad with Ginger-Wasabi Dressing*

DAY 6

Breakfast   Sunny-Side-Up Eggs and Veggie Sauté*

Snack   Guacamole* with sliced raw vegetables or flax crackers

Lunch   Thanksgiving-Style Quinoa-Stuffed Acorn Squash*

Snack   Vegetable Alkalizer Juice*

Dinner   Thai-Spiced Lentil Soup*
Mixed baby greens salad with Ginger-Mint Dressing*

DAY 7

Breakfast   Pumpkin Granola* with Almond Milk*

Snack   Green and/or black olives

Lunch   Egg salad on avocado half or in lettuce wraps
Handful of Jilz Gluten Free Crackerz

Snack   Chocolaty Avocado Pudding*

Dinner   Baked red snapper with Basil Herb Sauce*
Watercress Salad*

Breakfast

BREAKFAST IS THE MOST important meal of the day because it gives you the fuel you need to stay energetic all day long. If you skip breakfast, your blood-sugar levels can get out of balance, which may cause you to experience energy swings and, in turn, to crave sugar and caffeine to compensate for drops in your energy. The appetizing and nourishing breakfast recipes you'll find here—from Sun-Dried Tomato and Asparagus Quiche to Lemon-Blueberry Waffles—will not only light up your taste buds but help you start your day with greater vitality and focus.

"You determine how you will feel throughout each day by the type of breakfast you eat. You can produce inefficiency in yourself by eating too little food or too much of the wrong kind of food. Your breakfast establishes how readily your body can produce energy."

—ADELLE DAVIS

Sun-Dried Tomato and Asparagus Quiche

6 servings

Filling Ingredients:

6–7 eggs

2 tablespoons water

2–3 tablespoons olive oil or coconut oil for sautéing

4–5 cloves garlic, minced

½ teaspoon sea salt, divided

20 small asparagus, chopped into ¼-inch pieces (discard bottom quarter of stems)

¼ teaspoon black pepper

½ cup (packed) sun-dried tomatoes, chopped

Crust Ingredients:

1½ cups almond meal

¾ cup teff flour or any gluten-free flour (except corn or white rice)

½ teaspoon sea salt

¼ teaspoon black pepper

2 tablespoons fresh rosemary, minced

2 tablespoons water

⅓ cup olive oil

1 egg

Crust Directions: Preheat the oven to 400°F. Grease a pie dish generously with oil, and set aside. In a medium-sized bowl, whisk together the almond meal, the teff flour (or your choice of gluten-free flour), sea salt, pepper, and rosemary.

In a separate small bowl, whisk together the water, oil, and egg. Pour the wet ingredients into the dry and combine well. Pat this batter into the greased pie dish using your hands, spreading it evenly around the bottom and up the sides. The crust should be about ⅛–¼-inch thick. Poke the entire crust with a fork to prevent bubbles when baking. Bake for 15 minutes.

Remove from the oven and let cool for about 5–10 minutes before adding the filling.

Filling Directions: In a large bowl, whisk together the eggs and water, and set aside.

Heat 2–3 tablespoons of olive oil in a skillet over medium heat and add the garlic and ¼ teaspoon of sea salt. Sauté for a couple of minutes or until the garlic starts to release its aroma. Add the asparagus and another ¼ teaspoon sea salt and black pepper, and sauté for a couple minutes more. Add the sun-dried tomatoes and sauté for about 2–3 minutes more. Remove skillet from the heat and let cool for a couple of minutes.

Add the asparagus and sun-dried tomato mixture to the egg mixture, combine well, and pour into the crust. Bake for about 25–30 minutes or until the center is firm to the touch. Remove from the oven and let cool for about 10 minutes before cutting.

Spinach and Red Onion Frittata

6 servings

. . . .

Ingredients:

6–7	eggs
2	tablespoons water
2	tablespoons olive oil or butter for sautéing
½	red onion, diced
½	teaspoon sea salt
1	cup (packed) fresh spinach
¼	teaspoon black pepper
	Salsa or sliced avocado (optional)

Directions: Preheat oven to broil. In a medium-sized mixing bowl, whisk together the eggs and water, and set aside.

Place olive oil or butter in a well-seasoned 12-inch cast iron skillet over medium heat and sauté the diced red onions and sea salt for a couple of minutes. Add the spinach and give it a quick stir. Pour the egg mixture into the pan and stir one more time. Cook for about 4–5 minutes or until the egg mixture starts to set on the bottom.

Using an oven mitt, remove the skillet from the burner and place in the oven to broil for about 4–5 minutes or until lightly browned and fluffy. Remove from the oven and let cool for a couple of minutes before slicing. Enjoy warm, topped with salsa and/or sliced avocado.

Broccoli and Yellow-Onion Egg Muffins

6 servings

. . . .

Ingredients:

6	eggs
2	tablespoons coconut milk
¼	cup broccoli, finely chopped
¼	cup yellow onion, finely diced
1	tablespoon grapeseed oil
2	scallions, white and green parts finely sliced
½	teaspoon sea salt
¼	teaspoon black pepper
	Silicone muffin tin or muffin tin liners
	Coconut oil spray for muffin tin

Directions: Preheat oven to 350°F. In a large mixing bowl, whisk together the eggs and coconut milk.

Heat 1 tablespoon of grapeseed oil in a medium-sized skillet over medium heat and sauté broccoli and onion for about 2–3 minutes to cook slightly. Add the sautéed broccoli and onions to the egg mixture, and stir in the scallions, sea salt, and black pepper.

Liberally grease the muffin tin with coconut oil or coconut oil spray or use liners. Pour the batter into each cup, and bake for about 20–30 minutes or until the muffins have cooked and set. Cooking times will vary, so keep an eye on them. Remove from the tin and let cool on a cooling rack or eat warm.

POACHED EGGS AND TURKEY-BACON SALAD

2 servings

. . . .

Salad Ingredients:

½ package turkey bacon, diced
1 tablespoon olive oil
½ cup red onion, chopped
1 red bell pepper, diced
4 eggs
3 cups arugula
   Silicone egg-poaching cups (optional)
   Coconut or olive oil spray for egg-poaching cups

Dressing Ingredients:

⅓ cup olive oil
1 tablespoon raw apple cider vinegar
3–5 drops liquid stevia
3 sprigs fresh thyme, minced
   Sea salt and black pepper to taste

Directions: Heat 1 tablespoon of olive oil in a large skillet over medium heat. Add diced turkey bacon, red onion, and bell pepper. Sauté until onions and peppers are tender and bacon is browned a bit.

While turkey mixture is cooking, make the dressing, whisking together all the ingredients. Also wash and dry the arugula.

If using silicone egg-poaching cups, lightly spray with coconut or olive oil spray. In a pan that is wide enough to fit all of the egg poachers, add enough water for them to float. Bring to a boil and then reduce heat to a low simmer. Carefully crack open eggs, without breaking the yolks, into the egg-poaching cups and place in the water. Cover the pot to trap the steam and cook the top of the eggs.

If you do not have poaching cups, crack each egg into a small measuring cup or bowl and carefully slide the egg directly into a pot of gently simmering water (about 2 inches deep or enough to cover eggs); leave pot uncovered. Poach eggs to desired yolk consistency (3–5 minutes) and remove with a slotted spoon.

While the eggs are poaching, assemble the arugula in each bowl. Sprinkle the turkey-bacon mixture over the arugula and top with a poached egg. Drizzle dressing over the salads. Add more salt and fresh cracked pepper if needed.

MIXED VEGETABLE BREAKFAST SCRAMBLE

2–3 servings

. . . .

Ingredients:

2	tablespoons olive oil
4	cloves garlic, minced
2	tablespoons fresh ginger, minced
½	yellow onion, sliced into half moons
2	carrots, small dice
1	teaspoon smoked paprika
1	teaspoon cumin
¼	teaspoon sea salt
⅛	teaspoon black pepper
1	cup butternut squash, cut in small cubes
1	zucchini, cut into matchsticks
1	yellow squash, cut into matchsticks
2	tablespoons Raw Coconut Aminos or ½ teaspoon sea salt
1	tablespoon raw apple cider vinegar
4	tablespoons water, divided
2	cups kale, chopped
	Juice of 1 lemon or lime
¼	toasted pumpkin seeds (optional, p. 30)

Directions: Heat oil in a large, deep skillet over medium heat. Add garlic, ginger, onion, carrots, spices, salt, and pepper. Sauté for several minutes, until garlic and onions become fragrant. Add butternut squash, zucchini, yellow squash, Coconut Aminos (or salt), vinegar, and 2 tablespoons water. Cover tightly. Steam for 5 minutes or until butternut squash is soft. Remove lid, add kale, give a quick stir, and add 2 tablespoons water. Cover and cook until kale softens. Stir in lemon or lime juice and pumpkin seeds.

SUNNY-SIDE-UP EGGS AND VEGGIE SAUTÉ

1 serving

. . . .

Ingredients:

2	eggs
1	teaspoon olive oil
1	fresh chive, chopped
½	red bell pepper, chopped
½	jalapeño, seeded and finely chopped (optional)
½	yellow squash, diced
½	zucchini, diced
3	fresh basil leaves, chopped
	Sea salt and black pepper to taste

Directions: Heat olive oil in a large skillet over medium-low heat. Add chives, bell pepper, jalapeño, squash, zucchini, basil, sea salt, and black pepper. Sauté until vegetables are tender.

When tender, move vegetable mixture to one side of the pan and crack eggs onto the other side, keeping yolks intact. Cook until whites are no longer runny and yolks are cooked to your desired doneness (over easy, medium, or hard).

PUMPKIN-PIE-SPICED OATMEAL

4 servings

. . . .

Ingredients:

1   can pumpkin puree
2   cups water
2   cups almond milk
1   teaspoon vanilla extract
1   teaspoon pumpkin pie spice or ½ teaspoon cinnamon, ¼ teaspoon nutmeg, ¼ teaspoon ground cloves, and ¼ teaspoon cardamom
¼   teaspoon sea salt
2   cups gluten-free rolled oats
3   tablespoons xylitol or 15–18 drops liquid stevia, depending on preference
¼   cup pumpkin seeds or slivered almonds for garnish
2–4 tablespoons full-fat coconut milk to drizzle in cooked oatmeal

Directions: In a large saucepan, over high heat, combine the pumpkin puree, water, almond milk, vanilla, spices, and sea salt, and bring to a boil. Add the oats and give mixture a quick stir. Lower heat to a simmer, cover, and let simmer for about 15–20 minutes, stirring occasionally.

When the oatmeal is cooked, stir in the xylitol or stevia. Serve drizzled with coconut milk and garnished with pumpkin seeds or slivered almonds. (If the coconut milk is solid, it will liquefy when added to the hot cereal.)

BLUEBERRY-COCONUT QUINOA PORRIDGE

3 servings

. . . .

Ingredients:

1   cup uncooked quinoa
3   cups coconut milk
1   dash of vanilla extract
¼   teaspoon sea salt
1   teaspoon cinnamon
2   tablespoons almond butter
5–6 drops liquid stevia
¼   cup shredded coconut
½   cup fresh blueberries
¼   cup slivered almonds

Directions: Bring quinoa, coconut milk, vanilla, and sea salt to a boil. Reduce heat to low and simmer for about 15 minutes.

Stir in cinnamon, almond butter, and stevia until well combined. Add shredded coconut and blueberries, and cook until porridge is desired consistency. You may need to add water to make it creamier.

When desired consistency is reached, remove from heat, garnish with slivered almonds, and serve.

Oatmeal Breakfast Bake

4–6 servings

· ·

Ingredients:

2	cups gluten-free oats
2	cups gluten-free puffed cereal (millet, amaranth, etc., but not corn or white rice)
1	teaspoon baking powder
½	teaspoon fine sea salt
1	teaspoon ground cinnamon
1	cup vanilla almond milk
1	can coconut milk
½	cup nut butter (almond or pecan)
4	tablespoons xylitol or 10–24 drops liquid stevia
1½	cups berries (blueberries, raspberries, blackberries, or strawberries)
½	cup raw pecans or walnuts, chopped (optional)
	Coconut oil spray for baking dish
	Extra nondairy milk for topping

Directions: Preheat oven to 350°F and place one of the racks in the middle position.

Place the oats, puffed cereal, baking powder, sea salt, and cinnamon into a large mixing bowl and stir until thoroughly combined.

In a blender, place the almond milk, coconut milk, nut butter, and xylitol or stevia. Blend until creamy. Pour blended ingredients into dry ingredients and mix until well combined. If using large berries, such as strawberries, cut into bite-sized pieces. Stir in berries and nuts.

Spray a 9 x 12-inch baking dish with coconut oil spray and pour in the oatmeal mixture. Bake for 45–50 minutes or until firm to the touch and starting to turn golden brown on top.

Cut into squares and serve warm in a bowl with a drizzle of nondairy milk on top.

Almond Chai-Spiced Porridge

3 servings

. . . .

Ingredients:

1	tablespoon coconut oil
1	small green apple, small dice
¼	teaspoon sea salt
½	cup gluten-free rolled oats
¼	cup flaxseeds
½	cup quinoa flakes
2	tablespoons shredded coconut
1	teaspoon ground ginger
1	tablespoon ground cinnamon
½	teaspoon ground cardamom
¼	teaspoon ground cloves
3	cups vanilla almond milk, plus additional for garnish
1	cup water
1	tablespoon vanilla extract
2–3	tablespoons xylitol
5+	drops liquid stevia
¼	cup slivered almonds, plus extra for garnish

Directions: In a medium-sized saucepan, heat the coconut oil and add the chopped apple and ¼ teaspoon sea salt. Sauté for a couple of minutes to break down the apples.

Stir in the oats, flaxseeds, quinoa flakes, shredded coconut, and all of the dry spices (ginger, cinnamon, cardamom, and cloves).

Add the almond milk, water, and vanilla, and bring to a boil. Reduce heat to low, cover, and let the porridge simmer for about 10–15 minutes, stirring about every couple of minutes to prevent sticking and adding more liquid as necessary until the porridge is soft and creamy.

Stir in the xylitol, stevia, and slivered almonds. Taste to make sure the porridge is sweetened and spiced to your liking.

To serve, place ½ cup of porridge in each bowl, drizzle with additional almond milk, and sprinkle with a pinch of cinnamon and a small handful of slivered almonds.

CREAMY CINNAMON-COCONUT BUCKWHEAT PORRIDGE

3 servings

. . . .

Ingredients:

½   cup untoasted buckwheat groats

3   cups vanilla or plain coconut milk

1   cup water

¼   teaspoon sea salt

1   teaspoon vanilla extract

1   tablespoon cinnamon

2–3 tablespoons xylitol

    Up to 5 drops liquid stevia

¼   cup shredded coconut (use a brand with large flakes)

Directions: Rinse the buckwheat in a fine-mesh strainer until the water runs clear. Place buckwheat in a large saucepan with the coconut milk, 1 cup of water, and sea salt. Bring to a boil, reduce heat to low, and cover. Let simmer for about 20–25 minutes, stirring occasionally.

Add the vanilla, cinnamon, xylitol, and stevia, and let simmer for another 5 minutes. Stir in shredded coconut flakes, and taste for seasoning.

RASPBERRY-ALMOND AMARANTH AND TEFF PORRIDGE

3–4 servings

. . . .

Ingredients:

¾   cup amaranth

¼   cup teff

3½   cups water or nondairy milk

1¼   cups fresh raspberries, divided

¼   teaspoon sea salt

1   teaspoon vanilla extract

2   tablespoons xylitol and 10–12 drops liquid stevia

½   cup shredded coconut

¼   cup slivered almonds, plus extra for garnish

    Cinnamon, nutmeg, or shredded coconut for garnish

Directions: Rinse amaranth and teff in a fine-mesh strainer or tea strainer and place in a large saucepan with 3½ cups water or nondairy milk. Add 1 cup raspberries and sea salt to the saucepan and bring to a boil. Reduce heat to low, cover, and simmer for about 20 minutes, stirring periodically to prevent pot from overflowing and grain from sticking. After 20 minutes, check pot and add more water (or nondairy milk) if needed. Stir in vanilla, xylitol, and stevia. Simmer 5–10 minutes, stirring occasionally.

When grain is cooked and has reached desired consistency, stir in the shredded coconut and almonds. Garnish with ¼ cup berries, almonds, and a sprinkle of cinnamon, nutmeg, or coconut.

Pumpkin Granola

4–5 cups

....

Ingredients:

½   cup raw pumpkin seeds

½   cup raw sunflower seeds

½   cup raw slivered almonds

½   cup raw pecans, chopped

½   cup quinoa flakes

½   cup shredded coconut

½   cup xylitol, grind into finer powder

1   teaspoon ground cinnamon

1   tablespoon maca (optional)

1   teaspoon sea salt

¼   cup coconut oil, melted

1   teaspoon vanilla extract

½   cup pumpkin puree (canned)

¼   cup applesauce

     Coconut oil spray for baking sheet

Directions: Preheat oven to 300°F. Place all dry ingredients in large bowl and mix well. Melt coconut oil in saucepan over low heat. Then stir in the vanilla, pumpkin puree, and applesauce. Remove pan from burner, pour mixture into the dry ingredients, and stir well. Line baking sheet with parchment paper and spray with coconut oil. Spread granola mixture onto sheet and bake at 300°F for 20 minutes. Stir well to allow granola to cook evenly. Bake for another 10–15 minutes. Remove from oven and allow to cool for 20 minutes or until granola is hardened, then break into chunks. (Or place in refrigerator after it's cooled and before breaking it up, which helps it stick together better.) Enjoy as a snack as well as for breakfast.

Pumpkin-Spiced Pancakes

2 servings

....

Ingredients:

½   cup pumpkin puree (canned)

½   cup coconut milk (canned)

3   eggs

8   drops liquid stevia

1   tablespoon vanilla extract

1   teaspoon raw apple cider vinegar

¼   cup coconut flour

¼   cup tapioca flour

¼   cup ground flaxseed meal

1   tablespoon xylitol

½   teaspoon baking soda

¼   teaspoon sea salt

2   teaspoons cinnamon

½   teaspoon ground ginger

¼   teaspoon ground cloves

     Coconut oil spray for skillet

Directions: In medium-sized mixing bowl, whisk together pumpkin puree, coconut milk, eggs, apple cider vinegar, stevia, and vanilla until smooth. In a separate bowl, using a clean whisk, combine coconut flour, tapioca flour, flaxseed meal, xylitol, baking soda, sea salt, cinnamon, ginger, and cloves. Add this mixture to wet ingredients. Mix until thoroughly combined.

Heat a skillet over medium-low heat. Spray with coconut oil spray. Pour ¼ cup batter at a time onto skillet. Cook each side 3–5 minutes until lightly browned. (Be sure to cook 3–5 minutes. If you flip too soon, they won't hold together.) Serve topped with organic butter or ghee.

Gluten-Free Coconut-Raspberry Pancakes

4 servings

· ·

Pancake Ingredients:

1   cup brown rice flour
⅓   cup, plus 3 tablespoons, tapioca flour
2   tablespoons xylitol
1½   teaspoon baking powder
½   teaspoon baking soda
½   teaspoon sea salt
½   teaspoon xanthan gum
2   eggs
1   teaspoon vanilla extract
1¼   cups coconut milk
3   tablespoons grapeseed oil
¼   cup shredded coconut
1   cup raspberries
         Coconut oil spray for skillet

Coconut "Syrup" Ingredients:

         Zest and juice of 1 medium lemon
¼   cup coconut cream
¼   cup blueberries
¼   teaspoon sea salt
10   drops liquid stevia

"Syrup" Directions: Blend all of the syrup ingredients in a food processor or blender.

Pancake Directions: In a small bowl, mix together all of the dry ingredients.

In a medium-sized bowl, whisk together the eggs, vanilla, coconut milk, and oil. Add the dry ingredients to the wet mixture, and whisk until well combined and there are no lumps. Gently stir in the raspberries.

Heat a skillet over medium heat and spray with coconut oil spray. Pour about ¼ cup batter at a time onto the skillet, and cook each side for about 1–2 minutes until golden brown. Top with Coconut Syrup.

LEEK AND ONION QUICHE

6 servings

. . . .

Filling Ingredients:

6–7 eggs

2 tablespoons water

2–3 tablespoons olive oil for sautéing

3–4 cloves garlic, minced

1 cup yellow onion, small dice

½ teaspoon sea salt, divided

1 cup leek, thinly sliced into half moons (white and pale-green parts only)

⅛ teaspoon black pepper

Crust Ingredients:

1½ cups almond meal

½ cup teff flour or any gluten-free flour (except corn or white rice)

½ teaspoon sea salt

¼ teaspoon black pepper

2 tablespoons fresh rosemary, minced

2 tablespoons water

⅓ cup olive oil

Coconut or olive oil spray for pie dish

Crust Directions: Preheat oven to 400ºF. Spray a pie dish generously with coconut or olive oil spray and set aside.

In a medium-sized bowl, whisk together the almond meal, teff flour (or gluten-free flour of your choice), ½ teaspoon sea salt, ¼ teaspoon pepper, and fresh rosemary.

In a separate small bowl, mix the water and olive oil. Pour into the bowl of dry ingredients and combine well. Pat this batter into the greased pie dish, using your hands to spread it evenly around the bottom and up the sides. The crust should be about ⅛–¼-inch thick. Poke the entire crust with a fork to prevent bubbles when baking. Bake for 15 minutes.

Remove from the oven and let cool for about 5–10 minutes before adding the filling.

Filling Directions: In a large bowl, whisk together the eggs and water, and set aside.

Heat a skillet over medium heat with 2–3 table-spoons of olive oil, and add the garlic, onions, and ¼ teaspoon of sea salt. Sauté for a couple of minutes until the onions start to soften. Add the leeks, another ¼ teaspoon of sea salt, and the black pepper, and sauté for a couple minutes more.

Gently stir the leek, garlic, and onion mixture into the egg mixture and pour into the prepared crust. Bake for about 30 minutes or until the center is firm to the touch. Remove from oven and let cool for about 10 minutes before cutting.

Gluten-Free French Toast with Fresh Berry "Syrup"

6–8 servings

. . . .

French Toast Ingredients:

1   cup coconut milk

¼   teaspoon sea salt

3   eggs

1   heaping teaspoon ground cinnamon (more if you love cinnamon)

1   tablespoon vanilla extract

5–6   drops liquid stevia or 1 tablespoon xylitol

6–8   slices gluten-free bread (Almost Sourdough Bread, see page 185; or Sami's Millet & Flax Bread)

     Coconut oil or butter for skillet

Berry "Syrup" Ingredients (makes 1 cup):

     Zest of 1 lemon (optional)

1   cup fresh berries of choice

¼   cup water

¼   teaspoon sea salt

2–3   drops liquid stevia or ½ tablespoon xylitol

1   heaping teaspoon arrowroot flour

Berry "Syrup" Directions: Prepare syrup before cooking the French toast. Blend all of the syrup ingredients in a blender until smooth. Pour into a small saucepan and heat over medium heat, stirring continuously for several minutes until syrup starts to thicken. Pour into a glass container and let cool. (Syrup may also be used over waffles.)

French Toast Directions: Whisk together the coconut milk, sea salt, eggs, cinnamon, vanilla, and stevia or xylitol in a large bowl, and pour the mixture into a large rectangular baking dish. Place the bread in the mixture, and let soak for at least 10 minutes or up to an hour.

After the bread has soaked, coat a skillet or griddle with coconut oil or butter and heat skillet over medium heat. When skillet is hot, cook French toast on each side until golden brown. Serve warm with a spread of butter and drizzle of berry syrup.

Variation: If you have the time to double dip, try this delicious variation: after frying each piece of bread, dip the cooked pieces back into the egg mixture and fry again.

LEMON-BLUEBERRY WAFFLES

4–5 servings

. . . .

Waffle Ingredients:

- ¾ cup brown rice flour
- ¼ cup almond meal
- ¼ cup, plus 2 tablespoons, arrowroot flour
- 1 teaspoon baking powder
- ⅛ teaspoon sea salt
- 2 tablespoons xylitol or 10–12 drops liquid stevia

    Zest and juice of 1 lemon
- ¾ cup coconut milk
- 2 tablespoons grapeseed or safflower oil
- 2 eggs
- 1 teaspoon vanilla extract
- 1½ cups blueberries

    Coconut oil spray for waffle iron

Coconut "Syrup" Ingredients:

    Zest and juice of 1 medium lemon
- ¼ cup coconut cream
- ¼ cup blueberries
- ¼ teaspoon sea salt
- 10 drops liquid stevia (more if desired)

"Syrup" Directions: Blend all of the syrup ingredients in a food processor or blender.

Waffle Directions: Preheat waffle iron. In a large mixing bowl, whisk together the rice flour, almond meal, arrowroot, baking powder, sea salt, and xylitol until well combined and free of lumps (if using stevia, you will add it later). Zest the lemon into the bowl, grating the entire yellow surface layer, and whisk it into the dry mixture.

In a separate bowl, whisk together the lemon juice, coconut milk, grapeseed or safflower oil, eggs, vanilla, and stevia (if you're using it instead of xylitol). Pour the wet ingredients into the dry and mix until completely combined. Gently stir the blueberries into the batter.

For each waffle, spray the heated waffle iron surface with coconut oil spray. Pour the batter, about ⅓ cup at a time, into the center of the waffle iron and cook according to your iron's instructions. Gently remove waffles from the iron. Serve with Coconut Syrup. If you would like to warm up your waffles before serving, heat the syrup in a small saucepan over low heat and drizzle over the waffles.

Dressings, Dips, and Sauces

I LOVE DRESSINGS and sauces on my food. They add pizzazz and color to even the most simple meal or snack. With the healthy recipes in this section, you can still enjoy dips, dressings, and sauces without having to feel guilty or worry about putting on extra pounds. The delicious dressings are also a nice change from basic olive oil and fresh lemon. And when you're feeling hungry between meals, don't forget that the dips in this cookbook make great snacks along with sliced raw veggies, with a slice of gluten-free bread from my Breads and Snacks section, or with gluten-free crackers made of the grains or seeds on my "Foods to Eat" list (page 18).

"In the process of improving our diets, we all have an opportunity to increase our respect for our own bodies, as well as the body of the planet as a whole, through nourishing ourselves optimally with high-quality food."

—CHRISTIANE NORTHRUP, MD

Spinach-Artichoke Dip

4–6 servings

. . . .

Dip Ingredients:

1   (10-ounce) bag frozen spinach
1   (15-ounce) can artichokes, packed in water, chopped
2   tablespoons olive oil
1   yellow onion, sliced into half moons
½   teaspoon sea salt, divided
    Black pepper to taste
    Batch of "cream cheese"

"Cream Cheese" Ingredients:

1½ cups raw sunflower seeds
4   cloves garlic
    Juice of 2 lemons
2   tablespoons raw apple cider vinegar
½   teaspoon sea salt
½   cup water

Directions for "Cream Cheese": To start, create cream cheese by blending the sunflower seeds, garlic, lemon juice, raw apple cider vinegar, sea salt, and water in a high-powered blender until smooth and creamy. If it needs more liquid, add water until the consistency is similar to a thick sauce.

Directions for Dip: Heat 2 tablespoons of olive oil in a large skillet over medium-high heat. When hot, add the sliced onions and ¼ teaspoon sea salt. Sauté for a couple of minutes until onions start to break down and soften.

Add the frozen spinach and sauté until the spinach starts to soften, about another 2 minutes. Add the artichokes and the remaining ¼ teaspoon of sea salt, and sauté for about 2–3 minutes more.

Add the cream cheese to the skillet and mix well. Continue to sauté until the spinach is cooked and all the ingredients are nicely incorporated. Add black pepper to taste, and taste for seasoning.

Enjoy with sliced raw veggies, such as jicama, carrots, or cucumber slices, or with gluten-free crackers.

Hempseed Ranch Dip

Makes 3 cups

. . . .

Ingredients:

- ¾ cup olive oil
- ¼ cup fresh lemon juice
- 2 tablespoons Raw Coconut Aminos
- ½ cup water
- ½ cup raw sunflower seeds
- 1 cup raw hempseeds
- 3 cloves garlic
- 1–2 tablespoons jalapeño pepper, seeded and chopped (optional)
- 1 teaspoon sea salt
- ½ teaspoon black pepper
- ¼ cup fresh dill, chopped
- ¼ cup fresh scallions, white and green parts chopped
- ¼ cup fresh cilantro, chopped

Directions: Place all ingredients (except the fresh herbs) in a blender. Start blending on low speed and gradually increase, scraping down the sides as necessary. Blend until smooth and creamy, adding a little water if the mixture is too thick and isn't blending well.

Add the fresh herbs and blend briefly again. If you blend too long once the herbs have been added, the dip will turn green. Enjoy with sliced raw vegetables, gluten-free crackers, or as a salad dressing.

Homemade Ketchup

1–2 servings

. . . .

Ingredients:

- ¼ cup tomato paste (canned)
- 1 tablespoon raw apple cider vinegar
- 4 drops liquid stevia
- ¼ teaspoon sea salt
- ¼ teaspoon black pepper
- 3–4 dashes hot sauce (optional)
- 2 tablespoons water

Directions: Combine all of the ingredients in a bowl and whisk with a fork. Enjoy with sweet potato fries or on a burger.

VEGAN MAYONNAISE

Makes 1½ cups

. . . .

Ingredients:

1   cup safflower oil or grapeseed oil
½   cup full-fat coconut milk (not lite)
½   teaspoon sea salt
1   teaspoon dry mustard
    Juice of 1 lemon
1   tablespoon raw apple cider vinegar

Directions: Place the oil, coconut milk, sea salt, and dry mustard in a blender. In a small bowl or measuring cup, combine the lemon juice and raw apple cider vinegar.

Start the blender on low speed and slowly pour in the lemon juice and apple cider vinegar mixture, and blend until the mayonnaise starts to thicken. Taste for salt.

Transfer to a glass container with a tight-fitting lid and store in the refrigerator for up to 2 weeks.

HOMEMADE MAYONNAISE

Makes 2 cups

. . . .

Ingredients:

2   eggs
¼   teaspoon sea salt
1   teaspoon dry mustard powder or 2 tea-
    spoons mustard
2   tablespoons raw apple cider vinegar
2   cups grapeseed oil

Directions: In a blender, add the eggs, sea salt, mustard powder (or mustard), and raw apple cider vinegar. Start blending at the lowest speed, gradually drizzle in the oil, and blend until the mayonnaise starts to thicken.

Transfer to a glass container with a tight-fitting lid and store in the refrigerator for up to 2 weeks.

Note: Once refrigerated, the mayonnaise will solidify. Before using, leave at room temperature for 10–15 minutes to liquefy.

Sun-dried Tomato and Walnut Pesto

Makes 4 cups

. . . .

Ingredients:

3   cups (packed) fresh basil leaves

1   cup sun-dried tomatoes in oil (no need to drain)

4–5 cloves garlic

1   cup raw walnuts

¼   cup olive oil

     Juice of 2 lemons

1   teaspoon sea salt

¼   teaspoon black pepper

Directions: Place all of the ingredients in a food processor or blender and blend into a smooth paste. Enjoy this as a dip with veggies or as a pesto sauce for gluten-free pasta.

Note: This freezes well, so I like to make a big batch and store half of it in the freezer.

Basil Herb Sauce

2 servings

. . . .

Ingredients:

½   cup olive oil

1   tablespoon fresh lemon juice

1   cup (packed) fresh basil leaves

2   tablespoons fresh mint leaves, minced

2–3 cloves garlic

¾   teaspoon sea salt

¼   teaspoon black pepper

¼   teaspoon red pepper flakes (optional)

Directions: Place all of the ingredients in a blender, starting with the liquids, and blend until smooth. Enjoy over chicken, fish, gluten-free pasta, or veggies.

Italian Dressing

Makes 1 cup

. . . .

Ingredients:

¾ cup olive oil

¼ cup raw apple cider vinegar

2 tablespoons water

1 teaspoon garlic powder

1 teaspoon onion powder

1 teaspoon dried parsley

2 teaspoons dried oregano

¼ teaspoon dried basil

⅛ teaspoon sea salt

¼ teaspoon dried thyme

¼ teaspoon dried celery salt

¼ teaspoon black pepper

2–3 drops liquid stevia (optional)

Directions: In a bowl or 4-cup measuring cup, whisk together all of the ingredients. Taste for seasoning and add more salt if necessary.

Store in the refrigerator in an airtight glass jar for up to 2 weeks.

Ginger-Mint Dressing

Makes 1 cup

. . . .

Ingredients:

¼ cup (packed) fresh mint

1 1-inch piece fresh ginger, peeled and chopped

   Juice of 1 lime

¼ cup olive oil

2 tablespoons Raw Coconut Aminos

2 tablespoons blanched almonds

2 tablespoons water

¼ teaspoon sea salt

Directions: Place all of the ingredients into a high-powered blender. Start blending on low speed, gradually increasing to high, and blend until creamy.

Store in refrigerator in an airtight glass jar. Will stay fresh for about 1–2 weeks.

Use this dressing with the Tri-Color Quinoa Ginger-Mint Salad in the Salads section or on any salad of your choice.

CAESAR DRESSING

Makes 1 cup

. . . .

Ingredients:

¼   cup olive oil

     Juice of 1 large or 2 small lemons

¼   cup water, or more, depending on consistency desired

2   tablespoons Raw Coconut Aminos

2   heaping tablespoons raw almond butter

3   cloves garlic

1   tablespoon mustard (use spicy mustard if desired)

1   heaping tablespoon raw tahini

¼   teaspoon sea salt

Directions: Combine all ingredients in a blender, starting with the liquids, and blend until smooth.

Store in refrigerator in an airtight glass jar. Will stay fresh for about 1–2 weeks.

GINGER-WASABI DRESSING

Makes 1 cup

. . . .

Ingredients:

¼   cup ginger, peeled and chopped

2–3 cloves garlic

2   tablespoons raw apple cider vinegar

2   tablespoons Raw Coconut Aminos

¾   cup olive oil

¼   cup water

1   heaping tablespoon wasabi powder

2   drops stevia or 1 teaspoon xylitol (optional)

½   teaspoon sea salt

Directions: Wash and peel the ginger root, roughly chop, and place in blender along with garlic cloves. Add the remaining ingredients. Start blending on low speed, gradually increasing to high, and blend for about 1–2 minutes or until the dressing is smooth and creamy. Taste for seasoning.

Store in refrigerator in an airtight glass container. Will stay fresh for about 1–2 weeks.

Brazil Nut Parmesan "Cheese"

Makes 1 cup

Ingredients:

1   cup raw Brazil nuts (do not soak)
4–6 cloves garlic
1   teaspoon sea salt

Directions: Rinse the Brazil nuts in a colander and set aside. Place the garlic in a food processor and pulse for a couple seconds.

Add the Brazil nuts and sea salt, and pulse until the nuts crumble and get sticky. Store in an airtight container in the refrigerator or freezer.

Note: If you cannot handle eating raw garlic, try blanching the garlic (put cloves in boiling water for 5 minutes). This will slightly alter the taste of the "cheese."

Hummus

Makes 1 cup

Ingredients:

1   can garbanzo beans
3–4 cloves garlic
1–2 heaping tablespoons raw sesame tahini
1/3 cup olive oil
     Juice of 1 lemon
2   teaspoons ground cumin
2   teaspoons smoked paprika
     Small handful fresh cilantro, chopped, for garnish

Directions: Place the garlic in a food processor and pulse a few times. Scrape down the sides, add the remaining ingredients, and blend until smooth and creamy. Start with 1/3 cup olive oil and add a little more if you would like a creamier texture.

Serve garnished with fresh cilantro and enjoy with sliced raw vegetables or gluten-free crackers.

Spicy Guacamole

Makes 1 cup

. . . .

Ingredients:

2	avocados, peeled, pitted and mashed
½	teaspoon sea salt
	Juice of 1 lime
¼	red onion, finely diced
2–3	cloves garlic, minced
¼	jalapeño pepper, seeded and minced (optional)
¼	cup fresh cilantro, chopped
¼	teaspoon black pepper

Directions: Mash avocados in a medium-sized bowl and stir in the sea salt.

To loosen the juice in the lime, roll it on the counter with your palm. Cut lime in half and squeeze the juice into the bowl of mashed avocado.

Add the red onion, garlic, jalapeño pepper, and black pepper, and mash all of the ingredients together. Stir in the chopped cilantro and taste for seasoning. Enjoy as a dip for raw veggies, with gluten-free crackers, or added to your favorite wraps.

Lemon-Basil Pesto

Makes 1 cup

. . . .

Ingredients:

½	cup (packed) fresh basil
1	cup raw pine nuts, pumpkin seeds, or almonds
1	cup olive oil
	Juice of 2 lemons
1	teaspoon sea salt
4–6	cloves garlic

Directions: Place all of the ingredients in a high-powered blender. Starting on low speed and gradually increasing to high, blend for 1–2 minutes, scraping down the sides occasionally, until the mixture is smooth and creamy. Taste for seasoning.

Great to use with egg and chicken dishes, raw or cooked vegetables, and gluten-free grains, pasta, and crackers.

Carrot-Walnut or Carrot-Pecan Pâte

Makes 2 cups

. . . .

Ingredients:

2   cups carrots, roughly chopped

¼   cup cilantro, minced

1   cup raw walnuts or pecans, toasted

3–4   cloves garlic, blanched

2   tablespoons raw apple cider vinegar

1   teaspoon sea salt

1   cup cooking water from carrots

Directions: Bring a small pot of water to a boil and cook carrots until they are soft or can be pierced through with a fork (about 15–20 minutes, depending on cut size). Do not discard water.

Meanwhile, mince the cilantro and toast the walnuts or pecans. To toast, heat a skillet over low to medium heat, add the nuts, and stir continuously for about 3–5 minutes or until they begin to release their aroma. Be careful, as nuts will burn if not constantly moving. When toasted, place in a small bowl and set aside.

As soon as the carrots are done, add the garlic cloves to the pot of carrots and blanch for about 30 seconds. Turn off the heat, remove the carrots and garlic from the water with a mesh or slotted spoon, and place in a food processor. Save the cooking water to use later for making the pâte.

Add the nuts, raw apple cider vinegar, and sea salt to the food processor and begin to puree. Add the carrot cooking water a little at a time, until desired consistency is reached. Adjust seasonings to taste.

Pour the puree into a bowl and mix in the minced cilantro. Enjoy with sliced vegetables or gluten-free crackers.

Note: For a nut-free version, substitute 1 cup of white beans (such as great northern) for the walnuts.

Nacho "Cheese" Dip

Makes 4 cups

. . . .

Ingredients:

3   cups butternut squash, peeled, chopped

1–2   teaspoons sea salt

½   teaspoon black pepper

⅓   cup raw hempseeds

⅓   cup raw sunflower seeds

¾   cup almond milk

2   cloves garlic

1   tablespoon lemon juice

1   tablespoon raw apple cider vinegar

1   tablespoon smoked paprika

¼   teaspoon turmeric powder

      Grapeseed oil for baking sheet

Directions: Preheat oven to 350°F. Line a baking sheet with aluminum foil and lightly coat with grapeseed oil. Peel butternut squash and chop into ½-inch cubes. Place onto oiled baking sheet. Drizzle with a little more oil, and use your hands to coat all of the pieces. Sprinkle with 1–2 teaspoons salt (depending on your preference) and black pepper, and bake until tender, about 30 minutes. Stir halfway through cooking time.

When squash is cooked, remove from oven and let cool for 5 minutes. Place squash in blender along with the remaining ingredients. Start blending at low speed, gradually increasing to high, and blend for about 2–3 minutes or until smooth and creamy. You may need to add a little more almond milk to get the right consistency. Taste for seasoning.

Hot and Spicy Harissa

Makes ½ cup

. . . .

Ingredients:

¼   cup olive oil

1   red bell pepper, seeded and cut into 1-inch cubes

2   large cloves garlic, roughly chopped

1   tablespoon caraway seeds

1   tablespoon ground coriander

½   teaspoon red pepper flakes

¼   teaspoon sea salt

Directions: Heat ¼ cup olive oil over low heat in a medium-sized skillet and sauté all of the ingredients. Stir well to evenly combine. Cover and let simmer for about 5 minutes.

Remove skillet from burner, uncover, and let cool for a few minutes. Transfer mixture to a blender and blend on low speed, gradually increasing to high, for several minutes or until the sauce reaches desired consistency. Taste for seasoning.

Enjoy over chicken and lamb dishes or with vegetables.

Chimichurri

Makes ½ cup

....

Ingredients:

1   cup (packed) flat-leaf parsley leaves
    (½–1 bunch)
1   small clove garlic, finely minced
3   tablespoons unsweetened rice vinegar
4   teaspoons olive oil
½   teaspoon sea salt
¼   teaspoon cayenne pepper (optional)

Directions: Finely mince the parsley and garlic and place in a medium-sized bowl. Add the rice vinegar, olive oil, sea salt, and cayenne pepper, and stir to combine.

Use as a dipping sauce for chicken and red meat or as a topping for steamed vegetables.

Quick-and-Fresh Salsa

1– 2 servings

....

Ingredients:

1   cup cherry or mini plum tomatoes
2   tablespoons fresh cilantro, chopped
2   tablespoons red onion, roughly chopped
    Juice of 1 lime
¼   teaspoon sea salt
1   teaspoon raw apple cider vinegar
1   tablespoon jalapeño, seeded and roughly
    chopped (optional)

Directions: Place the tomatoes in a food processor and pulse about 5 times. If you like your salsa with a kick, add 1 tablespoon of the seeded and chopped jalapeños to the tomatoes before pulsing.

Add the remaining ingredients and pulse about 5 more times, scraping down the sides of the food processor at least once. Be careful not to over-pulse, as this will create too much liquid.

SALSA VERDE

Makes 1–2 cups

. . . .

Ingredients:

7   medium tomatillos, boiled until soft (use more tomatillos if only the tiny ones are available)

5   medium tomatoes

¾–1 bunch of cilantro

½   medium white onion

Juice of 3–4 limes

3   cloves garlic

¼   teaspoon sea salt

½–1 jalapeño, seeded and diced (adjust for desired spiciness)

1   avocado

Directions: Boil water in a small saucepan and cook tomatillos until soft. They will become somewhat darker in color after cooking.

In a blender, combine all ingredients (except the avocado) and blend until thoroughly mixed. Taste, and add more salt, garlic, or lime juice if desired. Transfer to a bowl.

Peel and dice one whole avocado and gently mix into the salsa. Refrigerate for at least 30 minutes before eating.

Enjoy with sliced raw veggies or in wraps.

CARROT-CUMIN SPREAD

Makes 1 cup

. . . .

Ingredients:

3   carrots, peeled and chopped (do not discard cooking water)

2   tablespoons fresh lemon juice

½   avocado

2   sprigs fresh dill, minced

2   sprigs fresh parsley, minced

1   teaspoon ground cumin

4   drops liquid stevia (optional)

Sea salt and black pepper to taste

Directions: Cut carrots into chunks and place in a saucepan with water to cover. Boil carrots until they are tender (about 10 minutes, depending on the size of the chunks), and save the carrot water.

In a blender, place the lemon juice and avocado first, and then add the remaining ingredients. Blend until smooth. If the spread is too thick, add 1 tablespoon of the carrot cooking water.

HORSERADISH

Makes 2 cups

. . . .

Ingredients:

1   cup horseradish, peeled and cubed
1   cup turnip, cubed (peeled if not organic)
½   teaspoon sea salt
½   cup raw apple cider vinegar

Directions: Peel the horseradish, chop into 1-inch cubes, and place in food processor. Pulse a couple of times to break it down.

Peel the turnip (if you are using an organic turnip, you do not need to peel it). Cut into 1-inch cubes and add to the food processor with the horseradish and pulse a few more times until broken down. You may need to stop a few times to scrape down the sides of the food processor with a spatula.

Add the sea salt, and while the food processor is running, slowly pour the raw apple cider vinegar through the feed tube. Start with ½ cup, and if it seems too dry, add another ¼ cup.

Enjoy horseradish in nori rolls or as a condiment with fish, chicken, or red meat.

Store in the refrigerator in an airtight glass container. If tightly sealed, this will stay fresh for several weeks.

Note: Be careful when smelling and handling this sauce. It is strong and potent and may be painful to breathe in.

OLIVE AND SUN-DRIED TOMATO TAPENADE

Makes 2 cups

. . . .

Ingredients:

2   cups Brazil Nut Parmesan "Cheese" (see page 81)
1   jar sun-dried tomatoes in oil (drained)
1   can green olives
1   can black olives

Directions: Place all ingredients in a blender and blend until smooth. Store in the refrigerator for up to 1 week.

TAHINI SAUCE

Makes 1–1½ cups

. . . .

Ingredients:

1–2 cloves garlic, minced
1   cup raw tahini butter
    Juice of ¼ lemon
1   tablespoon raw apple cider vinegar
½   teaspoon sea salt
¼   cup water

Directions: In a medium-sized mixing bowl, place garlic, tahini, lemon juice, raw apple cider vinegar, and sea salt. Mix with a fork or whisk while slowly adding the water a little at a time, until the sauce is smooth and a consistency that you like. Add more water if necessary.

Herbed Sunflower Spread

Makes 2 cups

. . . .

Ingredients:

1   cup raw sunflower seeds*

2   tablespoons olive oil

¼   yellow onion, small dice

1   ½-inch piece fresh jalapeño pepper,
       seeded for less spicy, small dice (optional)

2–3   cloves garlic, minced

½   cup water (plus more if needed)
       Juice of 1 medium lemon

1   tablespoon raw apple cider vinegar

1   tablespoon Raw Coconut Aminos (optional)

1   teaspoon sea salt

¼   teaspoon black pepper

¼   cup fresh dill, minced

¼   cup cilantro, minced

2   scallions, white and green parts minced

Directions: If soaking the sunflower seeds, place in a medium-sized bowl, cover with water, and let sit for 6–8 hours or overnight. Drain and rinse. If not soaking, rinse the seeds in a fine-mesh colander under cold running water as you swish them around with your hands.

Heat 2 tablespoons of olive oil in a medium-sized skillet and sauté onions, jalapeño, and garlic for about 2–3 minutes.

In a blender, place the sunflower seeds, water, lemon juice, raw apple cider vinegar, Coconut Aminos, onion/garlic/jalapeño mixture, sea salt, and black pepper. Blend until smooth and creamy. You may need to scrape down the sides with a spatula a couple times. Add more water if necessary, 1 tablespoon at a time.

When the mixture has reached a smooth con-sistency, add the minced dill, cilantro, and scallions and pulse 2–3 times until they are thoroughly mixed in. Be careful not to pulse too much or the cheese will turn green.

Enjoy with sliced raw vegetables or gluten-free crackers.

*Soaking the sunflower seeds is optional; how-ever, for this recipe soaking will make the cream cheese creamier.

Main Dishes

WHETHER YOU EAT RED MEAT, poultry, or fish or are a vegetarian, you will find flavorful entrées here that will add variety to your diet as well as help provide the protein your body needs to repair and regenerate itself. Because of the high levels of toxins in our environment, I recommend eating small amounts of animal protein at a time. It's always a good idea to eat slowly and to sit and savor your meals. This aids digestion and helps counteract the stress that can build up throughout the day. But in our busy world, we sometimes have to eat on the go. If you're in a hurry and need to eat a piece of leftover cooked chicken or fish for a meal, add one of the sauces or dressings in this cookbook that you've prepared ahead of time to make it tastier and more balanced.

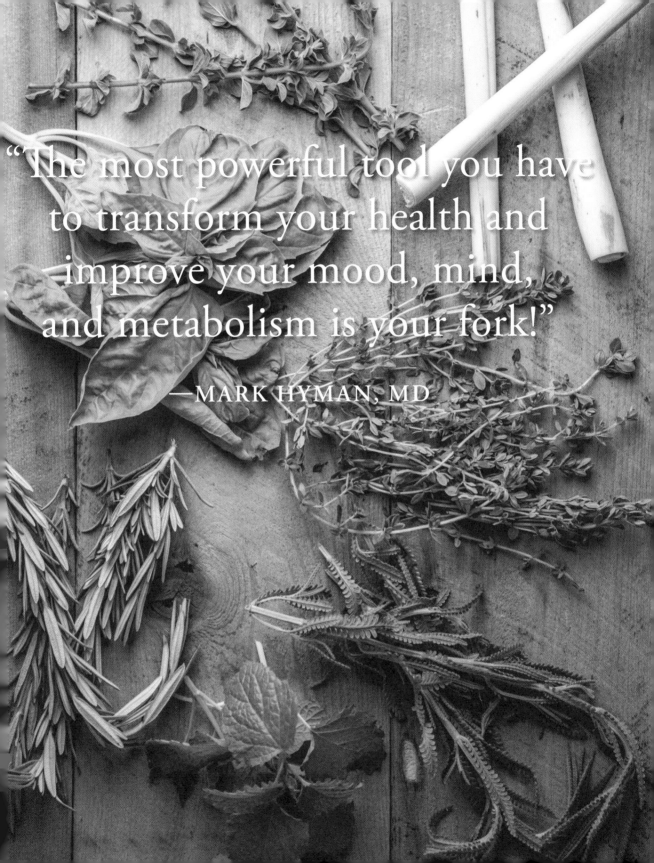

"The most powerful tool you have to transform your health and improve your mood, mind, and metabolism is your fork!"

—MARK HYMAN, MD

Zesty Baked Fish

2 servings

....

Ingredients:

½ pound fresh or frozen fillets of salmon, halibut, cod, etc. (cut in half)

¼ teaspoon sea salt

Pinch of black pepper

Zest and juice of 1 lemon

1 tablespoon butter

1 small handful of fresh cilantro, minced, for garnish

Olive oil spray for baking sheet

Directions: Preheat oven to 450°F. Thaw frozen fish ahead of time or place in a pan of cold water in sealed package until thawed (takes about 20–30 minutes). Line a baking sheet with foil and spray with olive oil spray. If fish has skin, place skin side down and season with sea salt and pepper.

Sprinkle the lemon zest on the fish, but do not squeeze the lemon juice on it just yet, as this will dry it out during cooking. Cut 1 tablespoon of butter in half and place a pat on each piece of fish. Bake until fish is cooked through, about 10–12 minutes.

While the fish is baking, mince the cilantro. Before serving, cut the lemon in half and squeeze onto the cooked fish. Garnish with minced cilantro.

Baked Cod or Salmon with Olive Tapenade

2–4 servings

....

Ingredients:

1 pound fresh cod fillet or salmon

1 tablespoon butter

Sea salt and black pepper to taste

Coconut oil spray for baking sheet

Olive Tapenade Ingredients:

3–4 cloves garlic, peeled and smashed

1 cup pitted black olives

¼ cup sun-dried tomatoes in oil

2 tablespoons capers

1 small bunch fresh cilantro

Juice of half a lemon

2 tablespoons olive oil

¼ teaspoon sea salt

¼ teaspoon red pepper flakes (optional)

Directions: Preheat oven to 450°F. Line baking sheet with parchment paper and spray lightly with oil. Place fish on baking sheet. Cut 1 tablespoon butter in half and place a pat on each piece of fish. Sprinkle with salt and pepper. Bake 12–15 minutes or until fish flakes with a fork.

While fish is baking, prepare the tapenade. Place smashed garlic cloves in food processor and pulse a couple times. Add olives, sun-dried tomatoes, capers, cilantro, lemon juice, olive oil, and sea salt. Pulse a couple more times or until everything is finely chopped and incorporated. Taste for seasoning. When the fish is finished cooking, top with the tapenade.

LEMON-LIME MARINATED SOLE

4 servings

· ·

Ingredients:

4   sole fillets (about 6 ounces each)

Marinade Ingredients:

    Zest and juice of 1 lemon

    Zest and juice of 1 lime

1   tablespoon olive oil

¼   teaspoon ground ginger

1   teaspoon smoked paprika

1   teaspoon ground cumin

1   tablespoon fresh mint, chopped

¼   teaspoon sea salt

    Olive oil spray for baking sheet

Directions: Mix marinade ingredients and pour into shallow dish. Place fillets in dish so they are covered with marinade; if not fully submerged, rub marinade all over them. Allow to marinate for at least 15 minutes and up to 1 hour.

Set the oven to broil. Line a baking sheet with foil and spray with olive oil. Remove fillets from marinade, place on baking sheet, and broil for 8–10 minutes or until they're no longer translucent.

MACADAMIA-CRUSTED TROUT, HALIBUT, OR MAHI-MAHI

4 servings

· ·

Ingredients:

4   fillets of trout, halibut, or mahi-mahi

1   tablespoon grapeseed oil for brushing on fish

    Coconut oil spray or grapeseed oil for baking dish

Crust Ingredients:

    Zest and juice of 1 large lemon

1   cup raw macadamia nuts, finely chopped

1   tablespoon fresh oregano, finely chopped

1   tablespoon fresh thyme, finely chopped

¼   cup parsley, finely chopped

1   clove garlic, minced

⅛   teaspoon sea salt

Directions: Preheat oven to 350°F. Spray a baking dish with coconut oil spray or brush with grapeseed oil. Place fillets in the dish and brush them with 1 tablespoon of grapeseed oil.

In a small bowl, mix all the crust ingredients to form a thick paste. With the back of a spoon or your hand, pat the mixture firmly and evenly onto the fillets. Bake until fish flakes with a fork, about 10 minutes, depending on the thickness of the fish.

Ginger Beef and Broccoli

4 servings

. . . .

Ingredients:

1	pound boneless sirloin steak, thinly sliced
1	tablespoon grapeseed oil
6	cups broccoli florets
1	heaping tablespoon arrowroot flour
3–4	scallions, finely chopped, for garnish
¼	cup raw sesame seeds

Sauce Ingredients:

1	cup vegetable broth
2	tablespoons sesame oil
1	tablespoon xylitol
2	teaspoons fresh ginger, peeled and minced
¼	teaspoon crushed red pepper (optional)
1	cup water
½	teaspoon sea salt

Directions: Whisk all of the sauce ingredients together in a small bowl. Pour half of the mixture into a large bowl, and add the sliced beef.

Heat grapeseed oil in a large skillet over medium heat and brown the steak strips, stirring constantly for about 5 minutes. Sauté in batches if the meat is too crowded so that it browns evenly.

Remove the steak from the skillet, transfer it to a bowl, and set aside.

In the same skillet, place the remaining sauce mixture and the broccoli florets, and cook covered until the broccoli is tender, but still crisp, about 2–5 minutes.

In a small bowl, mix and dissolve the arrowroot in 2 tablespoons of cold water. Pour this into the skillet and stir until the sauce starts to thicken. Add the steak, and stir until it is well coated. Garnish with chopped scallions and a sprinkle of sesame seeds.

MEXICAN-STYLE TURKEY MEATLOAF

3–4 servings

. . . .

Ingredients:

1   pound ground turkey

½   medium-sized onion, small dice

½   red bell pepper, small dice (optional)

3   cloves garlic, minced

½   jalapeño pepper, seeded, small dice (optional)

1   tablespoon olive oil

1   egg, beaten

2   tablespoons ground flaxseed meal

1   teaspoon sea salt, divided

1   teaspoon garlic powder

1   teaspoon ground cumin

1   teaspoon black pepper

1   teaspoon dried oregano

1   teaspoon fresh cilantro, minced

1   teaspoon paprika

    Olive oil to grease loaf pan

Directions: Preheat oven to 375°F. Lightly coat a loaf pan with olive oil and set aside.

Heat 1 tablespoon of olive oil in a medium-sized sauté pan, add ¼ teaspoon salt, and sauté the chopped onions, bell pepper, and garlic over medium heat for a couple of minutes. For a spicy meatloaf, sauté the jalapeño pepper along with these.

Remove veggies from heat, transfer to a bowl, and let cool for about 5 minutes.

Place the ground turkey in a large bowl and add the egg, flaxseed meal, remaining salt, spices, and sautéed vegetables. Mix thoroughly with your hands.

Place this mixture into the prepared loaf pan and bake for about 40 minutes or until the internal temperature reaches 165°F.

Remove meatloaf from the oven and let it cool slightly before removing it from the pan. Slice and serve garnished with fresh salsa (optional).

Turkey Meatballs and Collards

4 servings

Meatball Ingredients:

1	small onion
2	cloves garlic
6	large basil leaves
4	sprigs fresh thyme, needles removed and stem discarded
1	large sprig fresh rosemary, needles removed and stem discarded
5	sprigs parsley, chopped
	Handful arugula or spinach
1	pound ground turkey, dark or white meat
1	egg, lightly whisked
1	teaspoon sea salt
3	tablespoons grapeseed or olive oil
	Coconut or olive oil spray for baking sheet

Collards Ingredients:

5–6	collard leaves, cut in 1-inch pieces
½	yellow onion, sliced into half moons
1	tablespoon olive oil
2	tablespoons water
½	teaspoon sea salt, divided
1	tablespoon raw sesame seeds

Directions for Meatballs: Preheat oven to 375°F. Line a baking sheet with foil and spray with coconut or olive oil spray. Place the onion, garlic, fresh herbs, and arugula (or spinach) in a food processor. Pulse until very finely chopped.

Transfer to a large bowl and add turkey, egg, and 1 teaspoon sea salt. Mix gently to combine and, with your hands, form into golf-ball-size meatballs.

Heat grapeseed or olive oil in a large nonstick pan. Evenly brown the meatballs on all sides, about 3–4 minutes. You may need to do this in batches. Transfer to baking sheet and bake for about 20–25 minutes or until fully cooked.

Directions for Collards: While the meatballs are in the oven, slice the yellow onions into half moons. Heat 1 tablespoon of olive oil in a skillet over medium-high heat and sauté the onions with ¼ teaspoon of sea salt for a couple of minutes.

When the onions have started to break down, add the collards to the pan with about 2 tablespoons of water and another ¼ teaspoon of sea salt. Toss quickly, cover with a tight-fitting lid, and let the collards "steam" for about 2–3 minutes.

When done, sprinkle with sesame seeds and serve as a side dish to the meatballs.

Spiced Turkey Lettuce Wraps

4 servings

. . . .

Ingredients:

1	pound ground turkey, dark or white meat
1	tablespoon coconut oil for sautéing
¼	red onion, diced
1	1-inch piece fresh ginger root, minced
1	carrot, small dice
¼	teaspoon red pepper flakes (optional)
1	teaspoon dried oregano
1	teaspoon ground cumin
1	teaspoon chili powder (optional)
¼	teaspoon sea salt
2	scallions, white and green parts minced
2	tablespoons olive oil
2	tablespoons mustard
1	teaspoon raw apple cider vinegar
4	large romaine or butter lettuce leaves for the wraps

Directions: Heat 1 tablespoon of coconut oil in a nonstick skillet and sauté the red onion for 2–5 minutes.

Add the minced ginger, diced carrots, all of the spices—red pepper flakes, oregano, cumin, chili powder—and the sea salt, and sauté for about 2 minutes more. Transfer mixture to a bowl and set aside.

In the same pan, sauté the ground turkey over medium heat for 5–10 minutes or until the turkey is cooked through. Stir frequently and break the turkey into smaller-sized chunks as you go so that it cooks evenly.

Transfer the turkey mixture to the bowl of vegetables and stir in the minced scallions.

In a small bowl, whisk together the olive oil, mustard, and raw apple cider vinegar. Pour over the turkey mixture and mix well.

When the mixture has cooled slightly, place ⅓ cup of it in the center of each lettuce leaf. Wrap and eat like a taco.

BLACK BEAN QUESADILLAS

4–6 servings

. . . .

Quesadilla Ingredients:

1   can refried black beans*
¼   cup olive or coconut oil
½   red onion, small dice
3   cloves garlic, finely minced
        Sea salt and black pepper to taste
1   avocado, cut into small chunks
2–3   lettuce leaves, shredded
½   cup cherry tomatoes, quartered
1   batch Sunflower "Sour Cream"
1   package brown rice tortillas (no sugar)

"Sour Cream" Ingredients:

1   cup raw sunflower seeds
¼   cup cold water
¼   teaspoon sea salt
1   tablespoon raw apple cider vinegar
        Juice of 2 lemons

"Sour Cream" Directions: Place the sunflower seeds, water, salt, apple cider vinegar, and lemon juice in blender and puree 3–4 minutes or until smooth and creamy. Refrigerate unused portion up to 1 week.

Quesadilla Directions: Heat olive oil or coconut oil in a medium-sized skillet over medium heat. Add the onions, garlic, and a pinch of sea salt, and sauté for a couple of minutes, stirring frequently. Add the refried beans and sauté a couple minutes more, adding another pinch of sea salt and sprinkle of black pepper. When all the ingredients are thoroughly combined, transfer filling to a medium-sized bowl.

Place the prepared avocado, lettuce, tomatoes, and sour cream in separate small bowls next to the stove. Spread a thin layer of refried bean mixture on half of a tortilla, and spread a thin layer of the sunflower sour cream on the other half.

Brush a skillet that's large enough to fit 1 tortilla with ½–1 teaspoon of oil, and heat on a medium-high burner. When oil is hot, place quesadilla in the skillet, add the remaining toppings to the black bean side (tomatoes, avocado, lettuce). Don't add too much or it will be difficult to fold and flip the quesadilla. Let sit for about 30 seconds.

With a spatula, fold the sour cream side over the black bean side. Let sit for about 30 seconds. To flip quesadilla, gently place your free hand (the one not holding the spatula) on top of the quesadilla (carefully, as it will be hot), and place the spatula under the bottom of the quesadilla (from open end to closed end). Gently flip the quesadilla over and let sit for another minute or so, or until lightly browned. Remove from pan and place on cooling rack. Add a little more oil to the skillet if necessary to cook the next quesadilla.

While waiting for each quesadilla to brown, put the refried-bean mixture and sour cream on the next quesadilla. When all of the quesadillas are ready, cut each in half or in wedges with a serrated knife.

*See "Suggested Brands" list, page 33.

Spicy Lime Chicken Tacos with Cabbage Slaw

4 servings

. . . .

Chicken Ingredients:

1	pound chicken breasts, boneless
½	teaspoon cayenne pepper
½	teaspoon smoked paprika
½	teaspoon sea salt
½	teaspoon black pepper
¼	teaspoon nutmeg
1	(32-ounce) carton vegetable broth
1–2	tablespoons olive oil
1–2	tablespoons hot sauce
	Juice of 2 limes

Cabbage Slaw Ingredients:

2	cups finely shredded Napa cabbage
2	carrots, shredded
4	scallions, green and white parts thinly sliced
1	handful fresh cilantro, minced
¼	teaspoon sea salt
4	red radishes, cut in half and thinly sliced
	Zest and juice of 1 lime
2	tablespoons raw apple cider vinegar
2	tablespoons toasted sesame seeds

Cabbage Slaw Directions: Prepare the cabbage slaw while the chicken is cooking (see below). To toast sesame seeds, place them in a small skillet over low heat and stir continuously for about 3–5 minutes. Remove from burner when the seeds begin to release their aroma. Set aside. Place shredded Napa cabbage, carrots, sliced scallions, and minced cilantro in a large mixing bowl. Cut red radishes in half, place cut side down, thinly slice into half moons, and add to cabbage mixture. Sprinkle entire mixture with sea salt and massage in with your hands for about 1 minute. Add the lime zest and juice, raw apple cider vinegar, and toasted sesame seeds. Mix, and taste for seasoning. Set aside.

Chicken Directions: Place the chicken, cayenne pepper, smoked paprika, sea salt, pepper, and nutmeg in a large slow cooker. Pour in vegetable broth and cook on high for about 1–2 hours or until chicken is fully cooked. An alternate method is to cook the chicken in a roasting pan. Spray pan with olive oil, add the same ingredients, cover, and place in a 350°F oven for about 30–45 minutes. Cooking time will vary, depending on the thickness of each piece of chicken.

When chicken is cooked, remove from slow cooker or oven. Place on a cutting board or plate, let cool slightly, and shred with a fork. Heat 1–2 tablespoons of olive oil in a large skillet and briefly stir-fry the shredded chicken. Add the hot sauce and stir-fry a couple minutes more. Then add the lime juice and sauté another couple minutes.

To serve, make tacos or wraps with the shredded chicken and cabbage slaw, using Grain-Free Wraps (see page 185), romaine hearts, or butter-lettuce cups.

Variation: Spoon a cup of the cabbage slaw onto each plate and top with shredded chicken.

Apple-Spiced Turkey Burgers

4 servings

....

Ingredients:

1	pound ground turkey, white meat
½	cup Granny Smith apple, shredded (unpeeled if organic)
¼	cup handful fresh basil, minced
¼	cup red onion, minced
½	teaspoon sea salt
½	teaspoon smoked paprika
¼	teaspoon cinnamon
½	teaspoon ground cumin
4	large leaves romaine lettuce
1	beefsteak tomato, thinly sliced
1	ripe avocado, sliced
	Homemade Ketchup (see page 73)
	Olive oil spray for baking pan

Directions: Preheat oven to 350ºF. Line a baking sheet with parchment paper, and spray with olive oil spray. Place the ground turkey in a large bowl and add the apple, basil, red onion, and seasonings. Mix thoroughly with your hands to incorporate through, and make 4 round turkey patties. Place patties on prepared baking sheet and bake for about 12 minutes on each side or until the internal temperature reaches 165ºF.

Place each patty in the center of a lettuce leaf, top with sliced tomato, sliced avocado, and homemade ketchup or mustard, and then wrap and enjoy.

Vegan Sunburgers

8–10 servings

....

Ingredients:

1	cup raw sunflower seeds
1	cup raw pumpkin seeds
½	cup sun-dried tomatoes in oil (no need to drain)
1	cup carrot, grated
¼	teaspoon sea salt
1	teaspoon chili powder (optional)
1	teaspoon Italian herbs
½	teaspoon fresh garlic, chopped
3	tablespoons olive oil
8	large leaves of romaine or butter lettuce, or one leaf per serving
	Coconut or olive oil spray for baking sheet

Directions: Preheat oven to 350ºF. Line a baking sheet with parchment paper and lightly spray with coconut or olive oil spray.

Place all ingredients in a food processor and blend until a smooth batter is formed, scraping down the sides occasionally. Form the batter into patties and place on baking sheet.

Bake for 20–25 minutes or until patties are golden brown. Remove from baking sheet and place patties in lettuce wraps with sliced avocado and Homemade Ketchup.

EGGPLANT PIZZAS WITH BRAZIL NUT PARMESAN "CHEESE"

2 servings

....

Ingredients:

1	large eggplant, thinly sliced
1	teaspoon sea salt, divided
¼	cup olive oil, divided
¼	teaspoon black pepper
½	cup lacinato black kale, chopped into small bite-sized pieces
1	zucchini, sliced into thin rounds
1	tablespoon Raw Coconut Aminos
¼	cup tomato sauce
¼	cup fresh basil, chiffonade cut
½	cup Brazil Nut Parmesan "Cheese" (see page 81)
	Olive oil spray for baking sheet

Directions: Preheat oven to 350°F. Cut the eggplant into ½–1-inch rounds and place on a baking sheet in a single layer. Sprinkle with ½ teaspoon sea salt and let sit for about 10 minutes to remove some of the water from the eggplant. After 10 minutes, pat dry with a paper towel.

Remove eggplant from baking sheet and line the sheet with oiled parchment paper. Place the eggplant back on the sheet in a single layer. Drizzle with 2 tablespoons of olive oil, and sprinkle with a pinch of sea salt and ¼ teaspoon pepper. Bake for about 10 minutes or until eggplant starts to get soft.

While the eggplant is baking, heat 1 tablespoon olive oil in a medium-sized frying pan over medium heat and sauté the kale and zucchini rounds with the Coconut Aminos and a pinch of sea salt for about 2-3 minutes. Place in a small bowl and set aside.

Remove eggplant from the oven. Spread a layer of tomato sauce on top of each eggplant slice. Add about 2 tablespoons of the zucchini and kale mixture, some fresh basil, and a sprinkle of Brazil Nut Parmesan Cheese.

Drizzle with the remaining olive oil and sea salt, and bake for another 10 minutes. Remove from oven and serve hot or let pizzas cool on baking sheet to allow them to firm up.

Baked Mac and "Cheese"

4 servings

Ingredients:

½ (16-ounce) package of brown rice pasta or quinoa pasta (elbows or spirals)

2 cups butternut squash, peeled and cut in ½-inch cubes (small cubes cook quicker)

2–4 tablespoons olive oil

1 teaspoon sea salt, divided

4 cups broccoli, kale, or asparagus chopped into bite-sized pieces and blanched in pasta cooking water

1 cup coconut milk

½ cup raw hempseeds, rinsed

¼ cup raw sunflower seeds

4–5 cloves garlic

Juice of 1 lemon

1 tablespoon raw apple cider vinegar

2 teaspoons mustard

1 teaspoon dried basil

1 teaspoon smoked paprika

½ teaspoon dried turmeric

¼ teaspoon red pepper flakes

¼ teaspoon black pepper

¼ teaspoon hot sauce (optional)

Coconut oil spray for baking dish

Directions: Preheat oven to 350°F and line a baking sheet with parchment paper. Place squash on baking sheet, drizzle with 2–4 tablespoons olive oil, and sprinkle with ½ teaspoon sea salt. Using your hands, massage squash with oil and salt until pieces are evenly coated.

Place in oven on the middle rack and bake for about 20 minutes. Remove from oven and stir. If you can pierce with a fork, they are ready. If not, bake for another 5–10 minutes.

While squash is baking, chop broccoli, kale, or asparagus and set aside. Cook pasta according to package instructions. When there is about 1 minute of cooking time left, add the chopped vegetables to blanch them. Drain, rinse under cold water, and set aside in a large mixing bowl.

To make the "cheese" sauce, in a blender add the coconut milk first and then the cooked squash, hempseeds, sunflower seeds, garlic cloves, lemon juice, apple cider vinegar, ½ teaspoon sea salt, mustard, dried basil, paprika, turmeric, red pepper flakes, black pepper, and hot sauce. Starting on low speed and gradually increasing to high, blend for a couple of minutes or until smooth and creamy. Taste for seasoning and add more sea salt or spices if necessary.

Pour the sauce over noodles and vegetables, and stir until evenly combined. Spray a baking dish with coconut oil, and pour in the mixture. Bake on middle rack for about 20–25 minutes or until you see the outer edges start to brown. Let cool for about 5 minutes before cutting.

Variation: You can keep this recipe basic or load it up with other veggies as well. Get creative and add caramelized red onions, scallions, or fresh basil, etc.

SPICY BUCKWHEAT AND QUINOA STIR FRY

4 servings

. . . .

Stir Fry Ingredients:

¾	cup uncooked quinoa
¾	cup uncooked buckwheat
3	cups water
	Juice of 1 lime
1	tablespoon unsalted pasture butter
1	teaspoon hot sauce
1	teaspoon smoked paprika
¼	teaspoon black pepper
1	teaspoon sea salt, divided
1	red onion, diced
1	1-inch piece fresh ginger root, peeled and minced
3	cloves garlic, minced
	Cayenne pepper to taste (optional)
1	large carrot, diced
6	scallions, white and green parts thinly sliced
1–2	tablespoons coconut oil for sautéing
4	cups broccoli florets, chopped into bite-sized pieces
	Small handful fresh cilantro leaves, minced
½	cup slivered almonds

Sauce Ingredients:

	Juice of 1 lime
2	tablespoons Raw Coconut Aminos
1	tablespoon raw apple cider vinegar
1	tablespoon xylitol or 5 drops liquid stevia
¼	teaspoon hot sauce
½	teaspoon fine-ground sea salt

Directions: Rinse quinoa and buckwheat under cold running water in a fine-mesh strainer. Place in a medium-sized saucepan with 3 cups of water and the lime juice, butter, hot sauce, paprika, pepper, and ½ teaspoon sea salt. Bring to a boil, reduce heat to low, cover, and simmer for about 15–20 minutes or until all of the liquid has been absorbed. Set aside.

Combine all of the sauce ingredients and set aside.

Prepare stir-fry vegetables, keeping each one separate. Heat 1–2 tablespoons of coconut oil in a large skillet (or wok if you have one) over medium-high heat. When hot, add red onion, ginger, garlic, a pinch of sea salt, and cayenne (optional). Sauté for a couple of minutes, stirring constantly to prevent burning. Add diced carrots, scallions, and another pinch of sea salt, and sauté for a couple minutes more.

With the heat still at medium-high, add the cooked quinoa and buckwheat, chopped broccoli, and sauce to the skillet of sautéed vegetables. Stir to combine, cover with a lid, and let sit for about 3–8 minutes to "steam" the broccoli, which will keep it nice and crunchy, or steam longer if you prefer it softer. Uncover and remove skillet from heat. Stir in the cilantro and slivered almonds. Taste for seasoning.

THANKSGIVING-STYLE QUINOA-STUFFED ACORN SQUASH

2–4 servings

. . . .

Acorn Squash Ingredients:

2	acorn squash, washed, seeded and cut in half
2–4	tablespoons water
2	tablespoons olive or avocado oil
¼	teaspoon sea salt
¼	teaspoon black pepper

Stuffing Ingredients:

1	cup uncooked tri-color quinoa
2	cups vegetable broth
	Few pinches sea salt and black pepper
¼	cup olive or avocado oil, divided
¼	cup red onion, small dice
1	large carrot, small dice
1	stalk celery, small dice
½	teaspoon dried thyme
½	teaspoon dried rosemary
½	teaspoon dried sage
2	scallions, white and green parts chopped
2	tablespoons raw sunflower seeds

Directions: Preheat oven to 400°F. Place the squash cut side up in a baking dish with about 2–4 tablespoons of water in the bottom. Drizzle with 2 tablespoons olive or avocado oil, and sprinkle with ¼ teaspoon sea salt and ¼ teaspoon pepper. Bake for about 25–30 minutes.

Prepare the stuffing while the squash is baking. Rinse the quinoa and place in a medium saucepan with vegetable broth and a pinch of sea salt. Bring to a boil, reduce heat to low, cover, and simmer for about 15 minutes. Remove pan from heat and let sit covered for about 5 minutes to allow quinoa to unstick from the bottom of the pan. Transfer cooked quinoa to a medium-sized bowl.

Heat 1–2 tablespoons olive or avocado oil over medium heat in a medium-sized skillet and sauté onions, carrots, celery, dried herbs, and a pinch of sea salt and pepper for about 5 minutes. Add this mixture to the bowl of quinoa and stir to combine. Stir in the chopped scallions and sunflower seeds.

After the squash has baked for about 30 minutes, remove from oven and spoon stuffing mixture into each cavity. Drizzle with the remaining olive or avocado oil, and sprinkle with sea salt and pepper.

Bake for another 20–25 minutes or until the squash is fork-tender and the quinoa stuffing is slightly browned. Enjoy topped with Hot and Spicy Harissa (see page 86).

Kickin' Crab Cakes with Tartar Sauce

8–10 cakes

. . . .

Crab Cake Ingredients:

1	pound crabmeat, picked free of shells
⅓	cup almond meal
2	tablespoons coconut flour
3	scallions, white and green parts thinly sliced
½	cup red bell pepper, finely chopped
¼	cup red onion, minced
¼	cup Homemade Mayonnaise (see page 74)
1	egg
1	teaspoon dry mustard (optional)
1	teaspoon sea salt
¼	teaspoon garlic powder
¼	teaspoon black pepper
¼	teaspoon cayenne pepper (optional)
	Coconut or olive oil spray for baking sheet and broiling patties

Tartar Sauce Ingredients:

½	cup Homemade Mayonnaise (see page 74)
2	tablespoons capers
1	tablespoon raw apple cider vinegar
1	teaspoon mustard
¼	teaspoon sea salt
¼	teaspoon black pepper

Tartar Sauce Directions: Place all of the ingredients into a food processor or blender, and pulse or blend until the capers are finely chopped.

Crab Cake Directions: Pick through the crabmeat to make sure there are no shells, squeeze out any excess water (this step is very important), and place in a large mixing bowl. Add the almond meal, coconut flour, scallions, red bell pepper, minced red onion, mayo, egg, dry mustard, sea salt, garlic powder, black pepper, and cayenne pepper and mix well by hand.

Preheat the oven to broil. Line a baking sheet with foil or parchment paper and generously oil with coconut or olive oil spray.

Using your hands, form the crab mixture into patties. Place them on the greased baking sheet and spray the tops with coconut oil. Broil for about 8 minutes or until tops are golden brown.

Remove baking sheet from oven and carefully flip each crab cake. Spray tops with more oil and return to oven to broil for another 8 minutes. Enjoy with homemade tartar sauce.

COCONUT CURRY VEGETABLES

4 servings

....

Ingredients:

2   tablespoons coconut oil

½   yellow onion, small dice

2   cloves garlic, minced

1   ½-inch piece fresh ginger, peeled and minced

1   ½-inch piece fresh turmeric, peeled and minced

½   teaspoon sea salt, divided

1–2 tablespoons curry powder

2   teaspoons ground cumin

1   purple sweet potato, cut into small chunks

1   can coconut milk

1   cup vegetable broth

1   tablespoon Raw Coconut Aminos

1   tablespoon xylitol

1   stalk lemongrass, outer skin removed and cut into 1-inch pieces

2   cups broccoli florets, chopped into bite-sized pieces

2   cups cauliflower, chopped into bite-sized pieces

Directions: In a medium-sized saucepan, melt the coconut oil over medium heat. Add the onion, garlic, ginger, turmeric, and a pinch of sea salt, and sauté for a couple of minutes, until the vegetables start to sweat. Add the curry powder and cumin, and sauté for a couple minutes more. Add the chunked sweet potatoes and another pinch of sea salt, and sauté for about 2 more minutes.

Add the coconut milk, vegetable broth, Coconut Aminos, xylitol, and lemongrass, and bring to a boil. Reduce heat to low, cover, and simmer for about 10–12 minutes.

Add the chopped broccoli florets and cauliflower and simmer for a couple minutes more or until the potatoes are tender. Carefully remove lemongrass pieces with a slotted spoon. Taste for seasoning, adding more salt if necessary.

Enjoy over cooked quinoa, buckwheat, or brown rice.

Pad Thai Noodles with Grilled Salmon

4 servings

. . . .

Ingredients:

1   pound fresh salmon (more if desired)

1   teaspoon sea salt, divided

½   package gluten-free pad Thai noodles*

2   cups (packed) kale, chopped into small bite-sized pieces

¼   cup butter

5–6 cloves garlic, minced

     Coconut or olive oil spray for baking sheet

Directions: Preheat oven to 425°F. Line a baking sheet with parchment paper and lightly coat with coconut or olive oil spray.

Place the salmon, skin side down, on a baking sheet and sprinkle with ½ teaspoon sea salt. Bake for about 10–12 minutes, depending on thickness of fillet.

While the fish is baking, cook the noodles according to the package instructions.

Just before the noodles are done, add the 2 cups of kale to the pot and blanch for 5 seconds. Drain the noodles and the kale in a large colander and rinse with cold water. Let drain, transfer it to a large mixing bowl, and set aside.

To make the garlic butter sauce, melt the butter in a small skillet over medium heat and sauté the minced garlic with the remaining ½ teaspoon of salt for about 1–2 minutes, stirring constantly so you don't burn the garlic.

Pour the hot garlic butter sauce over the noodles and kale. Taste for seasoning and add more salt if necessary. Serve as a side with the salmon.

Note: Limit pasta dishes to only once a week.

*See "Suggested Brands" list, page 33.

Chicken-Vegetable Korma

4 servings

. . . .

Ingredients:

1	pound chicken tenders
3	tablespoons olive oil, divided
1¼	teaspoons sea salt, divided
¼	teaspoon black pepper
1	small onion, small dice
1	teaspoon fresh ginger, peeled and minced
4	cloves garlic, minced
1	red bell pepper, small dice
½	fresh jalapeño pepper, seeded and sliced (optional)
2	purple sweet potatoes, small dice
1	(4-ounce) can tomato sauce
1	cup coconut cream
1½	tablespoons curry powder
¼	cup slivered almonds
	Few sprigs of fresh cilantro, chopped, for garnish
	Olive oil spray for baking sheet

Directions: Preheat oven to 350°F. Line a baking sheet with parchment paper and spray with olive oil spray. Place chicken on sheet, drizzle with about 2 tablespoons of olive oil, and sprinkle with ¼ teaspoon sea salt and ¼ teaspoon pepper.

Bake for about 20–25 minutes or until chicken is fully cooked. When cool enough to handle, cut into bite-sized pieces and set aside.

Heat 1 tablespoon olive oil in a large skillet over medium heat. Stir in the onion, ginger, garlic, and ½ teaspoon sea salt, and sauté for a couple of minutes or until the vegetables become fragrant. Add the red bell pepper, jalapeño, and sweet potatoes, and sauté a couple of minutes more.

Add the tomato sauce, coconut cream, curry powder, and remaining sea salt. Stir to fully combine, cover with a tight-fitting lid, and reduce heat to low. Simmer for about 10 minutes or until the sweet potatoes are tender. Before serving, fold in the slivered almonds and garnish with cilantro.

Vegan Grain-Free Lasagna

4–6 servings

. . . .

Lasagna Ingredients:

1	purple sweet potato, sliced thin lengthwise
1	white sweet potato, sliced thin lengthwise
¼	cup, plus 1 tablespoon olive oil, divided
1	teaspoon sea salt, divided
½	teaspoon black pepper, divided
	Sunflower "cheese"
1	medium zucchini, sliced thin lengthwise
1	medium yellow squash, sliced thin lengthwise
1	red onion, thinly sliced into half moons
4	cups baby spinach, divided (reserve 2 cups as a bed for lasagna)
1	(9-ounce) jar tomato sauce

Sunflower "Cheese" Ingredients:

½	cup water (approximately)
1	cup raw sunflower seeds
2	tablespoons tahini
3	tablespoons arrowroot flour
	Juice of 2 lemons
1	tablespoon raw apple cider vinegar
1	teaspoon sea salt
3–4	garlic cloves

Note: Prep and cooking time about 1½ hours

Sunflower "Cheese" Directions: While sweet potatoes are baking, blend all ingredients until smooth and creamy, starting with ¼ cup water and adding up to ½ cup until mixture is thin enough to blend, but still thick enough to spread.

Lasagna Directions: Preheat oven to 350°F. Line baking sheet with parchment paper, coat with 2 tablespoons olive oil. Place sliced sweet potatoes on sheet, drizzle with 2 tablespoons olive oil, and sprinkle with ½ teaspoon salt and ¼ teaspoon pepper. Rub this all over potato slices. Bake until soft, about 20 minutes.

Heat 1 tablespoon olive oil in a medium-sized skillet over medium heat and sauté red onions with ¼ teaspoon sea salt for 3–5 minutes, until soft. Set aside. Prepare sunflower cheese.

When sweet potatoes are done, assemble lasagna in a 9 x 13-inch casserole dish. Spread a layer of tomato sauce along bottom of dish. Place one layer of zucchini and/or yellow squash over sauce and another layer of sweet potato on top of squash layer. Spread a layer of sunflower cheese on top of sweet potatoes, sprinkle some slivered red onions on top of that layer, then cover with spinach. Spoon some tomato sauce over the spinach. Repeat layering in the same order, beginning with zucchini/squash layer and finishing with spinach and tomato sauce.

If there's sunflower cheese left over, place a few dollops on top. Sprinkle with remaining ¼ teaspoon sea salt and ¼ teaspoon pepper. Place casserole dish on a baking sheet (to catch drippings) and bake uncovered for 45 minutes to 1 hour. Remove from oven and let cool for 30 minutes (this step is important, as it allows the cheese to set). Serve on a bed of fresh spinach.

SPAGHETTI-SQUASH PASTA WITH LAMB RED SAUCE

4 servings

Ingredients:

1   spaghetti squash, cut in half lengthwise, seeds removed
1   pound ground lamb
¾   teaspoon sea salt, divided
¼   teaspoon black pepper, plus 1 pinch, divided
2   tablespoons olive oil for sautéing
1   red onion, diced
4–5 cloves garlic, minced
1   1-inch piece of fresh ginger, peeled and minced
1   teaspoon dried oregano
¼   teaspoon red pepper flakes (optional)
1   can diced tomatoes with jalapeño peppers, with juice (jalapeño optional— can use plain diced tomatoes)
1   (24-ounce) jar good-quality red sauce
1   handful fresh basil leaves, finely sliced or chiffonade cut (see page 29)
    Olive oil for squash and for baking sheet

Directions: Preheat oven to 450°F. Line a baking sheet with parchment paper and coat with olive oil. Rub the flesh side of the spaghetti squash with olive oil and sprinkle with ¼ teaspoon sea salt and ¼ teaspoon black pepper. Place the squash flesh side down and roast for about 30–40 minutes or until it is done. You will know it is fully cooked when you can easily flake the squash into spaghetti-like pieces with a fork.

Meanwhile, heat 2 tablespoons olive oil in a large skillet. When hot, add the onion, garlic, and ginger, and sauté for a couple of minutes with ¼ teaspoon of sea salt. When the onion turns translucent, add the ground lamb, another ¼ teaspoon of sea salt and a pinch of black pepper, dried oregano, and red pepper flakes. Sauté, breaking the lamb into crumbles, until lightly browned, but not yet fully cooked, about 5 minutes.

Add the can of spicy diced tomatoes with juice and the red sauce. Cook for about 1–2 minutes more so that all of the flavors fully combine. Remove the skillet from the stove and place on a hot pad.

When the squash is cooked and cool enough to handle, use a fork to scrape the spaghetti strands from the flesh side (until you hit the skin) into a large bowl. Add the spicy lamb sauce and toss with the spaghetti squash.

Stir most of the basil into the squash and lamb, reserving some for garnish. Plate the spaghetti squash and sprinkle with fresh basil.

Note: If you don't like lamb, you can use ground turkey or beef instead.

STUFFED CORNISH HENS WITH WILD RICE

2 servings

. . . .

Cornish Hen Ingredients:

2	Cornish hens
3	tablespoons butter
2	tablespoons yellow onion, chopped
¼	cup celery, finely chopped
2	tablespoons slivered almonds
⅓	cup wild rice, uncooked
1	cup chicken broth
2	teaspoons fresh sage, chopped
2	teaspoons fresh thyme, chopped
½	teaspoon sea salt, divided
¼	teaspoon pepper
	Olive oil for brushing hens

Cranberry relish ingredients (optional):

1	(8-ounce) bag fresh cranberries
1	cup water
	Zest of one orange
¼	cup xylitol
	Pinch of sea salt
1	teaspoon ground cinnamon
⅛	teaspoon ground cloves

Cranberry Relish Directions: Place all of the ingredients into a medium-sized saucepan and bring to a boil. Cover, reduce heat to low, and simmer for about 30–40 minutes, stirring occasionally, until most of the liquid has evaporated. Use a wooden spoon to break up the cranberries and create a sauce-like texture.

Cornish Hen Directions: Preheat oven to 400°F. Melt butter in a saucepan over medium heat and sauté onions and celery until tender, about 5–10 minutes. Stir in almonds, wild rice, chicken broth, sage, thyme, ¼ teaspoon sea salt and ¼ teaspoon pepper. Bring to a boil. Reduce heat, cover, and cook until rice is tender and easily fluffed with a fork, about 45 minutes. Add more chicken broth as rice is cooking if necessary.

Remove giblets from inside Cornish hens. Rinse hens, including inside cavities, with cold water and pat dry with a paper towel. Season inside and outside with remaining sea salt and stuff with the rice mixture. Place hens breast side up in a roasting or baking pan with a lid. Brush with olive oil and bake covered for 30 minutes.

Baste hens with pan juices and continue baking uncovered for another hour or until hens are no longer pink, the juices run clear when thigh is pierced with a fork, and the internal temperature reaches 165°F.

Transfer hens to a plate and scoop out the rice mixture. Carve hens and serve with a side of rice and cranberry relish.

Bison-Stuffed Bell Peppers

4 servings

Ingredients:

4	yellow or red bell peppers, cut in half and seeded
1	pound ground bison
2–3	tablespoons olive oil
½	yellow onion, chopped
1	1-inch piece fresh ginger, peeled and minced
½	teaspoon sea salt, divided
1	zucchini, small dice
1	teaspoon dried basil
1	teaspoon dried thyme
1	cup (packed) fresh spinach
1	(15-ounce) can diced tomatoes, with juice
	Olive oil spray for baking sheet

Directions: Preheat oven to 350°F. Line a baking sheet with foil and spray with olive oil spray. Place the peppers face down and bake for about 10 minutes. Remove from oven and set aside.

Heat a medium-sized nonstick skillet over medium heat and add bison and a pinch of sea salt. (If you are not using a nonstick skillet, heat 1 tablespoon of olive oil in the skillet before cooking to prevent sticking.) Break the meat into crumbles, stirring frequently, and cook until they are evenly browned. Transfer to a large mixing bowl.

In the same skillet, heat 2 tablespoons of olive oil and add the onions, ginger, and a pinch of sea salt. Sauté mixture for a couple of minutes, stirring frequently.

Add the zucchini, basil and thyme, and another couple pinches of sea salt. Sauté a couple minutes more. Add the spinach, the can of diced tomatoes with juice, and another pinch of sea salt, and sauté for about 2–3 minutes.

Add this mixture to the bowl of cooked bison and stir to combine. Spoon mixture into each pepper cavity, and place the peppers, stuffed side up, on the baking sheet. Bake for another 10–15 minutes or until the stuffing starts to turn golden brown.

Note: If you can't find or don't like bison, you can use ground turkey, beef, or lamb instead.

Side Dishes

SIDE DISHES ARE A wonderful way to make a meal complete and help ensure that vegetables comprise 60 percent of your daily diet. If you are preparing a gluten-free grain meal or a meal with fish, poultry, red meat, or other protein, be sure to serve a salad or sautéed vegetable medley with it for optimal food combining and nutrient balance. You can look at my Four-Week Menu Plan at the beginning of this book for suggestions for combining sides with various main dishes—and feel free to mix and match. No matter what else is on your plate, these healthy sides will give your body and your taste buds a boost.

"The food we eat goes beyond its macronutrients of carbohydrates, fat, and protein. It's information. It interacts with and instructs our genome with every mouthful, changing genetic expression."

—DAVID PERLMUTTER, MD

Cauliflower Thai Rice

2–4 servings

. . . .

Ingredients:

1   head cauliflower
2   tablespoons olive oil or avocado oil
½   yellow onion, small dice
⅓   cup shredded coconut
     Couple pinches sea salt
     Pinch black pepper
     Fresh cilantro, parsley, or scallions, minced (optional)

Directions: Cut cauliflower in half, remove the core and leaves, and chop into small florets. Place in a food processor and pulse a couple times until the consistency looks similar to rice. Make sure not to over-pulse or it will turn into mush.

Heat 2 tablespoons of olive oil in a large skillet over medium heat and sauté onion and coconut with a pinch of sea salt for a couple of minutes. Add the cauliflower and another pinch of sea salt and a pinch of pepper, and sauté for about 5–10 minutes, stirring continuously.

Taste for seasoning and transfer to a large serving bowl. If you like, you may also toss in some minced fresh cilantro, parsley, or scallions before serving.

Garlic Mashed Cauliflower and Millet

Makes 4 cups

. . . .

Ingredients:

4   cups cauliflower, roughly chopped
1   cup uncooked millet
4–5   cloves garlic
2   tablespoons dried rosemary
½   yellow onion, roughly chopped
4   cups vegetable or chicken broth, or water
¼   teaspoon sea salt
¼   teaspoon black pepper
1–2   tablespoons olive oil
¼   cup chives, minced

Directions: Rinse the millet in a fine-mesh colander under cold running water until water runs clear. Cut cauliflower in half, remove the core and leaves, and roughly chop. In a deep saucepan, add all the ingredients (except chives and olive oil). Bring to a boil, reduce heat to low, cover, and let simmer for about 20–25 minutes.

Using a slotted spoon, transfer to a food processor, leaving behind most of the cooking liquid (if any is left). Add olive oil and blend until smooth. If you do not have a food processor, you can place the millet/cauliflower mixture into a large mixing bowl and mash with a potato masher. Taste for seasoning.

When it reaches the desired consistency, stir in the chives. Serve as you would a side of mashed potatoes.

Herbed Wild Rice Pilaf with Toasted Almonds

3–4 servings

....

Ingredients:

1   cup wild rice, uncooked
¼   cup unsalted butter
½   yellow onion, diced
3   stalks celery, diced
1   large (or 2 small) carrots, diced
1   1-inch piece fresh ginger, peeled and minced
1   teaspoon dried oregano
1   teaspoon dried basil
1   teaspoon dried thyme
3   cups chicken broth
¼   cup slivered almonds, toasted
     Salt and black pepper to taste

Directions: Melt the butter in a deep, large heavy skillet and sauté the onions, celery, carrots, and ginger with a pinch of sea salt for 1–2 minutes.

Add the wild rice, another pinch of sea salt, and the dried spices, and sauté for a couple minutes more. Add the chicken broth, cover, and simmer for 30–40 minutes or until rice is tender.

To toast the slivered almonds, heat a skillet over medium-low heat and dry sauté the almonds for about 3–5 minutes, stirring constantly to prevent burning. Set aside in a bowl.

Taste rice for seasoning, and add sea salt and pepper as needed. Fold in slivered almonds.

Sweet Potato Fries

2 servings

....

Ingredients:

1   purple, white, or orange sweet potato, thinly sliced in fry shapes
¼   cup grapeseed oil, divided
1   heaping tablespoon arrowroot or tapioca flour
¼   teaspoon sea salt
¼   teaspoon black pepper

Directions: Preheat oven to 425°F, with an oven rack at the lowest or next-to-lowest position. Spread 2 tablespoons grapeseed oil on a baking sheet with your hands or a brush. Cut sweet potato into thinly sliced fry shapes, keeping them roughly the same size for even cooking.

In a large mixing bowl, add the remaining 2 tablespoons grapeseed oil, arrowroot or tapioca flour, sea salt (¼–½ teaspoon depending on your preference), and pepper. Dip the fries in the mixture and coat them well, using your hands.

Spread fries out on baking sheet in a single layer, leaving a little space between them so they will be easy to flip.

Bake fries for about 15 minutes. Remove from the oven and flip the fries using a spatula. Return to oven and continue baking for about 10–15 minutes more or until they are crispy to your liking.

MACADAMIA-ROASTED BRUSSELS SPROUTS

2–4 servings

. . . .

Ingredients:

3	cups Brussels sprouts
¼	cup olive oil
1	teaspoon sea salt
½	teaspoon black pepper
	Zest and juice of 1 lemon
½	cup macadamia nuts, coarsely chopped

Directions: Preheat oven to 375 °F. To prepare the Brussels sprouts, remove any yellow or brown outer leaves, cut off the ends, and then cut in half lengthwise. Place on a baking sheet, drizzle with ¼ cup olive oil, and sprinkle with sea salt and pepper. Using your hands, massage the oil evenly onto the Brussels sprouts and spread it on entire baking sheet to prevent sticking.

Bake for about 15–20 minutes. Remove from oven and stir the Brussels sprouts to ensure even roasting. Bake for about 15–20 minutes more or until they are tender and can be pierced through with a fork.

While baking, wash and coarsely chop the macadamia nuts. When the Brussels sprouts are almost done, sprinkle the chopped nuts over them and bake for about another 1–2 minutes. Remove from oven, transfer to a bowl, and stir in the lemon zest and lemon juice. Serve warm.

TENDER COLLARDS AND ONIONS

1–2 servings

. . . .

Ingredients:

1	small bunch collards
½	yellow onion, sliced into half moons
1	clove garlic, minced
	Pinch of sea salt
1	tablespoon raw apple cider vinegar
2	tablespoons olive oil
2	tablespoons slivered almonds, pine nuts, or sunflower seeds (optional)

Directions: Rinse the collard greens, and while keeping them slightly damp, cut out the central ribs and stems. Slice the ribs and stems into small pieces, about ⅛–¼ inch, and set aside. Cut the leaves into ½-inch pieces.

Heat olive oil in a large skillet over medium-high heat and sauté the sliced onions, minced garlic, and pinch of sea salt for a couple of minutes. When the onions start to break down, add the sliced collard ribs and stems, and sauté for a couple minutes more.

Add the collard leaves and apple cider vinegar. Cover the pan with a tight-fitting lid and cook for about 2 more minutes or until the collards are nice and soft.

Remove from heat and toss in 2 tablespoons of slivered almonds, pine nuts, or sunflower seeds (optional). Serve warm.

Purple Cabbage Vegetable Medley

Makes 4 cups

Vegetable Medley Ingredients:

½   head of purple cabbage, thinly sliced
2   teaspoons olive oil
2   red bell peppers or zucchinis, thinly sliced
1   red onion, thinly sliced
     Small handful of fresh cilantro, minced
¼   cup raw sunflower seeds, toasted

Dressing Ingredients:

¼   cup olive oil
1   teaspoon raw apple cider vinegar
     Zest and juice of 1 lemon
⅛   teaspoon sea salt
¼   teaspoon black pepper

Dressing Directions: In a small bowl, whisk together ¼ cup olive oil, raw apple cider vinegar, lemon zest and juice, sea salt, and black pepper. Set aside.

Vegetable Medley Directions: After peeling off the outer layer of the purple cabbage, wash and thinly slice. Add 2 teaspoons of olive oil to a medium skillet and sauté the cabbage, red bell peppers or zucchini, and red onion for 5–10 minutes. Transfer to a medium-sized bowl.

Pour the dressing over the cabbage mixture. When it is cool to the touch, massage the dressing into the vegetables using your hands.

To toast the sunflower seeds, place them in a small skillet over low heat and stir continuously for about 3–5 minutes. Be careful, as seeds will burn quickly if not constantly moving. Remove from burner when the seeds begin to release their aroma.

Add the cilantro to the bowl with the cabbage mixture and lightly toss. Sprinkle with toasted sunflower seeds. Enjoy hot or cold.

Lemon-Roasted Asparagus

1–2 servings

....

Ingredients:

1	small bunch asparagus, tough ends trimmed
2	tablespoons olive oil
	Zest of 1 lemon
$1/8$	teaspoon fresh thyme, minced
$1/8$	teaspoon sea salt
$1/8$	teaspoon black pepper

Directions: Preheat oven to 350°F. Trim off the tough ends of the asparagus and discard, and place asparagus on a baking sheet.

Drizzle with olive oil and sprinkle with the zest of 1 lemon, thyme, sea salt, and black pepper. Using your hands, massage ingredients evenly onto the asparagus.

Bake for about 5–10 minutes or until cooked but still crunchy. Enjoy as a side with fish or meat entrée.

Steamed Baby Bok Choy

2 servings

....

Ingredients:

4	small heads of baby bok choy, left intact
1	tablespoon olive oil
$1/8$	teaspoon sea salt
$1/8$	teaspoon black pepper
1	tablespoon water
1	teaspoon brown rice vinegar

Directions: Leave the heads of the bok choy intact and rinse. Heat 1 tablespoon of olive oil in a medium-sized skillet over medium heat. When hot, add the bok choy, sea salt, black pepper, and 1 tablespoon of water.

Cover with a tight-fitting lid. Let steam for about 3 minutes. Remove skillet from heat and drizzle with brown rice vinegar. Serve warm.

ROASTED ROSEMARY VEGETABLES

4–6 servings

· ·

Ingredients:

1   carrot, cut into ½-inch chunks (unpeeled if organic)

½   rutabaga, cut into ½-inch chunks (unpeeled if organic)

2   yellow or red bell peppers, seeded, ½-inch cubes

1   bulb fennel, cut in half and thinly sliced

1   medium eggplant, thinly sliced lengthwise

½   yellow onion, large dice

3   shallots, finely diced

4–6 cloves garlic, minced

¼   cup fresh rosemary, minced

2–4 tablespoons olive oil, divided

1   teaspoon sea salt

     Zest and juice of 1 large lemon

¼   teaspoon black pepper

Directions: Preheat oven to 400°F. Place the prepared carrots, rutabaga, and peppers in a large mixing bowl.

Cut off the top of the fennel and end of the bulb. Cut it in half lengthwise and slice into thin strips. Cut the ends off the eggplant and slice lengthwise into thin strips. Place in bowl with cubed vegetables, shallots, and minced garlic.

After washing the fresh rosemary, remove the needles from the stems, mince to get ¼ cup, and add to the bowl. Add 2 tablespoons of oil, sea salt, lemon zest and juice, and black pepper. Toss well.

Oil a large glass baking dish with the remaining oil and add the vegetables. Bake for 20 minutes. Remove from the oven, stir the veggies, and continue baking for another 20–25 minutes.

Taste for seasoning. Serve warm.

QUINOA TABBOULEH

4 servings

. . . .

Tabbouleh Ingredients:

1   cup uncooked white quinoa
2   cups water or vegetable broth
    Pinch of sea salt
4–5 scallions, white and green parts finely sliced
1   cup cherry tomatoes, small chop
1   cup Persian cucumbers, small dice
1   handful fresh parsley, minced
1   handful fresh cilantro, minced
1   handful fresh mint, minced (optional)
½   cup toasted and salted pumpkin seeds or pine nuts

Dressing Ingredients:

¼   cup olive oil
    Juice of 2 lemons
3–4 cloves garlic, minced
½   teaspoon sea salt
¼   teaspoon black pepper

Dressing Directions: In a small bowl, whisk together the olive oil, lemon juice, minced garlic, ½ teaspoon sea salt, and ¼ teaspoon pepper. Set aside.

Tabbouleh Directions: Rinse the quinoa in a fine-mesh strainer and place in a small saucepan with 2 cups water or broth and a pinch of sea salt. Bring to a boil, reduce heat to low, cover, and let simmer for 15 minutes. Remove pan from heat, but keep the lid on for another 5 minutes to prevent quinoa from sticking to the bottom of the pan.

While quinoa is cooking, toast the pumpkin seeds or pine nuts by placing them in a small skillet over low heat and stirring continuously for about 3–5 minutes. Be careful, as they will burn quickly if not constantly moving. Remove from burner when the seeds begin to release their aroma, and sprinkle with salt.

In a small bowl, mix together the prepared scallions, tomatoes, cucumbers, and pumpkin seeds (or pine nuts). Set aside.

When the quinoa is cooked, fluff it in the saucepan with a fork while transferring it to a large bowl. Stir in the mixed vegetables and seeds/nuts, the fresh herbs (parsley, cilantro, and mint), and the dressing. Taste for seasoning.

Soups

SOUPS ARE ONE of my favorite things to eat. They can be hearty or light and are nourishing and satisfying. Soups are versatile too. They can be served before a main dish or be eaten with simply a salad or gluten-free crackers and a dip. And if you are eating a lot of cold or raw foods, soups are a nice change of pace. What I enjoy most about making soups is being creative and using the vegetables, herbs, or grains I have on hand. Whether it's Thai Coconut-Lentil Soup, Creamy Carrot Ginger, Roasted Beef Bone Marrow Broth, or any of the other soups in this section, you'll find an array of ideas and ingredients to get your own creative juices flowing.

"Your body has not forgotten how to heal—you just need to create the right environment for a long enough period of time to remove inflammation and infection."

—ANN BOROCH, CNC

Herbed Vegetable Puree

2–4 servings

. . . .

Ingredients:

4–6	cups of vegetables of your choice, coarsely chopped
2	tablespoons olive oil, divided
1	yellow onion, coarsely chopped
4	cups chicken or vegetable broth, divided
2	tablespoons fresh herbs of your choice, chopped, plus extra for garnish
¼	teaspoon sea salt
¼	teaspoon black pepper

Directions: Heat 1 tablespoon of olive oil in a stockpot and sauté the yellow onion for 5–10 minutes over low heat. Stir in the rest of the vegetables, 1 more tablespoon of olive oil, sea salt, pepper, herbs, and ½ cup of the chicken or vegetable broth. Cover and continue cooking over low heat until the vegetables are tender (time will vary, depending on type and size of vegetables used). When tender, add the rest of the broth and cook until heated.

Carefully pour soup mixture into a Vitamix or blender. Fill blender only half to three-quarters full so it doesn't overflow when blending. You may have to blend in 2 batches. Blend on the puree setting until smooth and creamy. Add salt and pepper to taste, and garnish with fresh herbs of your choice. Serve hot.

Variation: Instead of making a puree, you can make a regular vegetable soup by cutting the vegetables into bite-sized pieces.

Broccoli Pottage

2–4 servings

. . . .

Ingredients:

4	tablespoons butter
1½	pounds broccoli, roughly chopped
1	large onion, chopped
¼	teaspoon sea salt
¼	teaspoon ground black pepper
4	cups vegetable or chicken broth, or just enough to cover the vegetables
½	cup coconut or almond milk

Directions: Melt 4 tablespoons of butter in a heavy medium-sized pot over medium heat. Add broccoli, onion, sea salt, and pepper, and sauté until onion is translucent (approximately 6 minutes). Add broth and bring to a boil. Reduce heat to low, cover, and simmer until broccoli is tender, approximately 15 minutes. Pour in coconut or almond milk and heat for a couple of minutes.

Remove pot from heat and carefully pour soup mixture into a Vitamix or blender, filling it only half to three-quarters full to avoid overflowing when blending. You may have to blend in 2 batches. Blend using the puree setting. Taste for seasoning and add more salt and pepper if needed. Serve hot.

Tuscan White Bean Soup

4 servings

. . . .

Ingredients:

¼	cup olive oil
½	medium onion, small dice
2	cloves garlic, minced
1	carrot, small dice
1	stalk celery, small dice
¼	teaspoon dried thyme
¼	teaspoon dried basil
¼	teaspoon dried oregano
¼	teaspoon dried rosemary
¼	teaspoon sea salt
¼	teaspoon black pepper
6	cups cannellini beans (cooked), divided
3	cups vegetable broth, divided
1	(9⅓ ounce) can diced tomatoes, with juice
1	bay leaf
4	sprigs fresh parsley, chopped, for garnish

Directions: Heat oil in a 4-quart soup pot over medium heat. Add onion, garlic, carrots, celery, dried herbs (except bay leaf), salt, and pepper. Cook vegetables until tender, about 10 minutes.

Meanwhile, puree 2 cups of the beans with 1 cup of the vegetable broth. When vegetables are tender, add the pureed beans, remaining vegetable broth, remaining beans, can of diced tomatoes with juice, and bay leaf to the soup pot. Simmer for at least 10 minutes and up to 30 minutes, depending on size of vegetables. Taste for seasoning. Transfer to individual bowls and garnish with chopped parsley.

Hearty Chicken-Vegetable Soup

4–6 servings

. . . .

Ingredients:

2–3	chicken breasts (skin on)
2	tablespoons olive oil
1	large yellow onion, small dice
1	teaspoon sea salt
4–5	carrots, small dice
4–5	stalks celery, small dice
1	purple sweet potato, cut into small chunks
4	cups water
1	cup tomato sauce (optional)
1	bunch lacinato black kale, chopped
	Black pepper to taste
	Cooked millet or quinoa (optional)

Directions: Heat olive oil in a large soup pot over medium heat. Add the diced onion and sea salt, and sauté for a couple of minutes until the onions start to sweat. Add the carrots and celery, and sauté for a couple minutes more. Add the sweet potato, chicken breasts, water, and tomato sauce. Bring to a boil, reduce heat to low, cover, and simmer for about 1 hour.

When soup is finished cooking, remove chicken breasts from the pot. Let cool slightly, remove and discard skin, and cut into bite-sized pieces. Return chicken to soup pot. Season to taste.

This soup is delicious served with a few spoonfuls of cooked quinoa or millet in it. You may also garnish with chopped parsley.

Thai Coconut-Lentil Soup

4 servings

. . . .

Ingredients:

1½ cups split red lentils

1–2 tablespoons olive or coconut oil

1 large yellow onion, diced

2–4 cloves garlic, minced

1–2 inches of fresh ginger, peeled and minced

2 carrots, small dice

2 tablespoons red curry paste

½ teaspoon dried turmeric

1 teaspoon ground cumin

¼ teaspoon cinnamon

¼ teaspoon nutmeg

¼ teaspoon red pepper flakes (optional)

4 cups vegetable broth

1 can coconut milk

4 cups lacinato black kale, chopped

Sea salt and pepper to taste

Fresh cilantro or scallions, finely chopped

Directions: Rinse and drain the lentils. In a tall stockpot or a soup pot, heat the olive or coconut oil over medium heat. Sauté the onion, garlic, ginger, and a pinch of sea salt for 2–3 minutes or until the onion is translucent.

Add in the diced carrot and sauté for 2–3 minutes more. Add the red curry paste, turmeric, cumin, cinnamon, nutmeg, and red pepper flakes. Sauté for 2–3 more minutes.

Add the lentils, vegetable broth, and coconut milk. Cover and bring to a boil, reduce heat to low, and simmer for 10–12 minutes (or until the lentils are tender), stirring occasionally. When lentils are tender, stir in the chopped kale.

Season to taste. Garnish with fresh cilantro or scallions.

HERBED CAULIFLOWER SOUP

3–4 servings

. . . .

Ingredients:

1   head of cauliflower, chopped into 1-inch pieces
1   yellow onion, 1-inch dice
1   tablespoon olive oil
¼   teaspoon sea salt
¼   teaspoon black pepper
1   sprig fresh rosemary or 1 tablespoon dried
1   sprig fresh thyme or 1 tablespoon dried
4   cups vegetable or chicken broth
    Filtered water

Directions: Cut cauliflower in half, remove the core and leaves, and chop into 1-inch pieces. In a large stockpot, place chopped cauliflower, onions, olive oil, sea salt, black pepper, and dried herbs. If using fresh herbs, wait until soup is cooked before adding them.

Add 4 cups vegetable or chicken broth plus just enough water to cover the veggies. Bring to a boil, reduce heat to medium-low, and cover. Let simmer for about 10–15 minutes or until the cauliflower can be pierced with a fork.

Transfer soup to a blender. If you are using fresh herbs, remove stems and add leaves to blender. Start blending at low speed, gradually increasing to high, and blend until nice and creamy. Taste for seasoning, and add more sea salt and pepper if necessary.

CREAM OF ASPARAGUS SOUP

2–3 servings

. . . .

Ingredients:

1   bunch asparagus, tough ends trimmed
1   yellow onion, diced
½   can coconut milk (optional)
2   cups vegetable broth
¼   cup (packed) fresh basil
¼   teaspoon sea salt
¼   teaspoon black pepper

Directions: Trim off the tough ends of the asparagus and discard. Chop the spears into 1-inch pieces and place in a saucepan with diced onions.

Add the coconut milk and enough vegetable broth to just cover the vegetables (slightly more or less than 2 cups). Add the sea salt and pepper, and bring to a boil. Reduce heat to low, cover, and simmer for about 10–15 minutes.

Transfer the soup to a blender, add fresh basil, and blend until smooth and creamy. Season to taste.

LEEK AND ONION SOUP

4 servings

. . . .

Ingredients:

4	small leeks or 2 large, white and pale-green parts sliced
2	yellow onions, chopped
2	tablespoons olive oil
1	white sweet potato or rutabaga, diced
½	teaspoon sea salt
¼	teaspoon black pepper (or to taste)
4	cups vegetable broth
1	cup almond or other nondairy milk
1	tablespoon chives, chopped

Directions: Heat olive oil in a large saucepan over medium heat and add the leeks, onions, and sweet potatoes or rutabaga. Stir to coat the vegetables with the oil. Season with sea salt and pepper, cover the pan, and let vegetables sweat over very low heat for about 15 minutes.

Add the vegetable broth and nondairy milk, and bring to a simmer. Cover and let simmer gently for about 20 minutes or until vegetables are soft. Transfer to a blender, and blend until smooth and creamy. Add chopped chives, and season to taste.

CREAMY CARROT-GINGER SOUP

3–4 servings

. . . .

Ingredients:

9	carrots, roughly chopped
1	yellow onion, diced
1	1-inch piece of ginger, peeled and diced
1	can coconut milk
	Filtered water
	Sea salt to taste
	Raw walnut pieces, crumbled, for garnish

Directions: Place all ingredients (except walnuts) into a medium-sized saucepan with just enough water to cover the vegetables. Bring to a boil, reduce heat to low, cover, and simmer until vegetables are soft, about 15 minutes.

Transfer soup to a blender, and blend until smooth and creamy. Season to taste and garnish with a handful of crumbled walnut pieces.

Roasted Beef Bone Marrow Broth

4–6 servings

Ingredients:

1	pound grass-fed beef marrow bones (about 2)
½–1	teaspoon sea salt
¼	teaspoon black pepper
8	cups water
1	large carrot, roughly chopped
3–4	cloves garlic, smashed
1	onion, cut into large chunks
2	stalks celery, cut into chunks
1	handful fresh cilantro, chopped
1	sprig fresh rosemary

Directions: Preheat oven to 350°F. Place the bones on a baking sheet (with a lip to catch fat drippings), and sprinkle with sea salt and ¼ teaspoon pepper. Bake for 10–15 minutes.

Meanwhile, prepare the vegetables and the herbs.

When the bones are finished baking, place them and the remaining ingredients in a large slow cooker, along with any fat and juices that have dripped onto the baking sheet. Set slow cooker on low, and let simmer for 12–24 hours.

The longer you cook the broth, the more flavorful it gets and the more nutrients it draws from the bones. If you do not have a slow cooker, cook in a large stockpot over medium to low heat for 1–3 hours.

When done cooking, let cool slightly and remove the bones. Using a fine-mesh strainer, strain the vegetables and herbs from the broth.

Enjoy broth with Garlic-Rosemary Paleo Bread (see page 183) and unsalted pasture butter.

Note: Leftover broth can be placed in glass jars, filled about three-quarters full. When cooled, seal the jars and store in the freezer for up to several weeks. If you're a dog lover, you can treat your pet to a bone.

THAI-SPICED KABOCHA SQUASH SOUP

4 servings

Ingredients:

1   kabocha squash, peeled, seeded and cut into 1-inch chunks

2   tablespoons coconut oil

2   yellow onions, large dice

     Pinch of sea salt

1   can lite coconut milk

1   can full-fat coconut milk

3   teaspoons red Thai curry paste

⅛   teaspoon sea salt

     Filtered water

     Handful of raw pumpkin seeds, toasted

Directions: Heat the coconut oil in a large soup pot and sauté the onions with a pinch of sea salt until they start to sweat.

Add the kabocha squash, both cans of coconut milk, the red Thai curry paste, ⅛ teaspoon sea salt, and just enough water to cover vegetables. Bring to a boil, reduce heat to medium-low, cover, and simmer for about 20 minutes or until squash is tender enough to pierce with a fork.

Transfer the soup to a high-powered blender (you may have to do this in batches). Start blending at low speed, gradually increasing to high, and blend until smooth and creamy.

To toast the pumpkin seeds, place them in a small skillet over low heat and stir frequently for about 3–5 minutes. Remove from the burner when the seeds begin to release their aroma.

Taste for seasoning and add more sea salt or Thai-spiced paste if desired.

Serve garnished with toasted pumpkin seeds.

Turkey or Lamb Chili with Sunflower "Sour Cream"

Makes 1 very large pot

. . . .

Chili Ingredients:

1	pound ground turkey or lamb
4	tablespoons olive or coconut oil, divided
1	yellow onion, small dice
1	1-inch piece fresh ginger, peeled, minced
4–5	cloves garlic, minced
1	teaspoon sea salt, divided
1	teaspoon ground cumin
1	teaspoon smoked paprika
½	teaspoon coriander
¼	teaspoon cinnamon
¼	teaspoon black pepper
2	carrots, small dice
1	fennel bulb, small dice
2	stalks celery, small dice
2	orange bell peppers, small dice
4	cups vegetable broth
1	can diced tomatoes, with juice
4	scallions, white and green parts chopped
	Zest of 1 orange
1	avocado, sliced, for garnish

"Sour Cream" Ingredients:

1	cup raw sunflower seeds*
¼	cup cold water
¼	teaspoon sea salt
1	tablespoon raw apple cider vinegar
	Juice of 2 lemons

"Sour Cream" Directions: Place sunflower seeds, water, sea salt, apple cider vinegar, and lemon juice in a blender and puree for 3–4 minutes or until smooth and creamy (refrigerate any leftovers in an airtight container up to 1 week).

Chili Directions: Heat 2 tablespoons oil in a large soup pot over medium heat. Add onion, ginger, garlic, and ½ teaspoon sea salt. Sauté a couple minutes until vegetables start to sweat.

Add the dry spices and sauté a couple more minutes. Add carrot, fennel, celery, orange peppers, and ½ teaspoon sea salt, and sauté for another couple minutes. Add the vegetable broth and can of diced tomatoes with juice. Bring to a boil, reduce heat to low, cover, and simmer for about 10 minutes.

To prepare the turkey or lamb, heat 2 table-spoons oil in a medium-sized skillet and sauté the meat with a pinch of sea salt and ¼ teaspoon black pepper. Break it into crumbles so it cooks evenly, and cook until it's almost fully cooked.

Transfer meat to the soup pot after vegetables have cooked for 10 minutes, and continue cooking until meat is fully cooked and veggies are soft. Remove from heat and stir in the orange zest and scallions (save some for garnish). Serve with a dollop of sour cream, and garnish with sliced avocado and scallions.

*Soaking the sunflower seeds is optional; however, for this recipe soaking will make the sour cream creamier. If you choose to soak the seeds, refer to instructions on pages 28–29.

Salads

SALADS, LIKE SOUPS, are a great way to incorporate an assortment of vegetables and herbs into one meal. I enjoy salads most when the vegetables are shredded or chopped into small pieces. To save preparation time, cut up your unwashed vegetables ahead of time, maybe on a Sunday. When you're ready to make the salad, all you'll need to do is wash the vegetables and add them to the recipe. The salads that follow also draw on ingredients like beans, nuts, seeds, grains, chicken, fish, and eggs to create wholesome and refreshing meals. Experiment with your own fresh ingredients—and have fun!

"To control candida, you must change your diet."

—WILLIAM CROOK, MD

Tri-Color Quinoa Ginger-Mint Salad

2 servings

Salad Ingredients:

1	cup tri-color quinoa
2	cups vegetable broth
¼	teaspoon sea salt
2	tablespoons olive oil
	Juice of 1 lemon
4	cups leafy greens
1	carrot, shredded
1	small red beet, shredded or spiralized
¼	cup toasted almonds

Dressing Ingredients:

5	sprigs fresh mint
1	1-inch piece fresh ginger, peeled and chopped
	Juice of 1 lime
¼	cup olive oil
2	tablespoons Raw Coconut Aminos
2	tablespoons raw almonds
2	tablespoons water
¼	teaspoon sea salt

Dressing Directions: While quinoa is cooking, prepare the dressing. Place all of the ingredients in a high-powered blender and blend until creamy, starting on low speed and gradually increasing to high.

Salad Directions: Rinse the quinoa in a fine-mesh strainer and place in a small saucepan with the vegetable broth and sea salt. Bring to a boil, reduce heat to low, cover, and simmer for 15 minutes. Remove from heat and keep the lid on for another 5 minutes to prevent quinoa from sticking to the bottom of the pan. Add 2 tablespoons olive oil and lemon juice to cooked quinoa and fluff with a fork.

To serve, place a few spoonfuls of the quinoa in the bottom of each bowl and top with leafy greens, shredded carrots and beets, a sprinkle of almonds, and a drizzle of the salad dressing.

Red Quinoa Taco Salad

4 servings

. . . .

Ingredients:

1½	cups red quinoa
3	cups vegetable broth or water
¼	teaspoon sea salt
1–2	tablespoons olive oil
	Juice of 1 lime
2	tablespoons taco seasoning (see below)
1	can black beans
3–4	scallions, white and green parts chopped
3	tomatoes, chopped
½	red onion, diced
5	sprigs of fresh cilantro, chopped (more if desired)
1	avocado, chopped
4	cups mixed salad greens

Taco Seasoning Ingredients:

2	teaspoons chili powder
1½	teaspoons smoked paprika
1	teaspoon onion powder
½	teaspoon sea salt
½	teaspoon garlic powder
½	teaspoon cumin
½	teaspoon oregano
¼	teaspoon black pepper
¼	teaspoon cayenne pepper (optional)
¼	teaspoon red pepper flakes (optional)

Directions: Rinse quinoa in a fine-mesh strainer. Place in a small saucepan with the vegetable broth (or water) and sea salt, and bring to a boil. Reduce heat to low, cover, and simmer for 15–20 minutes. Remove from heat and keep the lid on for another 5 minutes to prevent quinoa from sticking to the bottom of the pan.

While quinoa is cooking, chop all your vegetables and toss them together (except for the avocado) in a large mixing bowl.

In a small bowl, combine all the taco seasoning ingredients.

When quinoa is cooked, fluff with a fork and stir in olive oil, lime juice, and taco seasoning. Add the black beans, chopped vegetables, cilantro, and avocado, and gently mix. Season to taste and serve over mixed greens.

CHEF'S SALAD

2 servings

. . . .

Salad Ingredients:

1	chicken breast, uncooked
	Olive oil
¼	teaspoon sea salt
¼	teaspoon black pepper
2	large hard-boiled eggs, cut into wedges
2	cups mixed salad greens
¼	cup Persian cucumbers, thinly sliced
¼	cup cherry tomatoes, cut in half
¼	cup red onion, thinly sliced
1	small carrot, grated (about ¼ cup)
¼	cup Brazil Nut Parmesan "Cheese" (see page 81)

Dressing Ingredients:

1	tablespoon minced fresh chives
2	tablespoons olive oil
1	tablespoon raw apple cider vinegar
2	teaspoons mustard powder
⅛	teaspoon sea salt
¼	teaspoon black pepper
2–4	drops liquid stevia (optional)

Dressing Directions: Place all of the dressing ingredients in a small bowl or measuring cup, and whisk briskly.

Salad Directions: Start by preparing the chicken breast. Preheat oven to 450°F. Line a baking dish with parchment paper and brush each side of the chicken breast with olive oil. Sprinkle with sea salt and pepper, place in baking dish, and bake for about 20 minutes or until the internal temperature reaches 165°F when a meat thermometer is inserted into the thickest part of the breast. Cooking time will vary, depending on the size of the breast. When fully cooked, remove from the oven and let rest for about 5 minutes before cutting into strips. Set aside.

To prepare the hard-boiled eggs, place the eggs in a single layer in a small saucepan. Add cold water to cover eggs by about 1 inch. Heat over high heat just to boiling and then remove from burner. Cover the pan and let the eggs stand in the hot water for about 12 minutes (about 9 minutes for medium-sized eggs, and 15 minutes for extra-large eggs). When the time is up, drain the hot water and cool eggs under cold running water or place them in a large bowl of ice water. Carefully peel the eggs and cut into wedges. Set aside.

To assemble the salads, arrange salad greens on two plates. Place cucumber slices, cherry tomatoes, and sliced red onion on top of the lettuce greens and sprinkle with grated carrot. Divide the chicken strips and hard-boiled egg wedges between the two plates and top with Brazil Nut Parmesan Cheese. Drizzle with dressing.

Roasted Butternut Squash and Marinated Red Onion Salad

4 servings

. . . .

Roasted Butternut Squash Ingredients:

1	butternut squash, cut into ½-inch cubes (skin may be left on)
	Olive oil for baking sheet
	Sea salt and black pepper to taste
½	cup sun-dried tomatoes in olive oil, sliced (no need to drain)
¼	cup pumpkin seeds or sunflower seeds
2	cups arugula, spinach, or mixed greens
1	cup Brazil Nut Parmesan "Cheese" (optional, see page 81)
	Lemon wedges for garnish

Marinated Red Onion Ingredients:

1	red onion, sliced into half moons
¾	cup raw apple cider vinegar
1	tablespoon xylitol or 5–6 drops liquid stevia
½	teaspoon sea salt
1	teaspoon dried thyme
1–2	cloves garlic, minced
3–4	whole cloves or ¼ teaspoon ground cloves
2	cups water

Marinade Directions (best prepared 2–3 hours in advance): In a small bowl, mix the raw apple cider vinegar, xylitol or stevia, sea salt, dried thyme, minced garlic, and cloves.

Peel the onion and cut off the ends. Cut in half lengthwise (along the onion ribs) and thinly slice into half moons. Blanch onions in a small saucepan with 2 cups of boiling water for 30 seconds, and quickly remove with a slotted spoon. Place them in the marinade and let soak for at least 30 minutes or up to 2–3 hours. Remove whole cloves before adding marinade to squash.

Roasted Butternut Squash Directions: Preheat oven to 375°F and generously oil a baking sheet. Peel squash if you prefer it that way. Cut into ½-inch cubes and place on oiled baking sheet. Drizzle squash with more olive oil and sprinkle with sea salt and pepper. Bake for about 20 minutes, stirring occasionally, until the squash is tender enough to easily pierce with a fork.

When the butternut squash and marinade are ready, toss together in a large mixing bowl along with the sliced sun-dried tomatoes and pumpkin or sunflower seeds. Taste for seasoning.

To serve, place a handful of arugula, spinach, or mixed greens on each plate and top with the butternut squash mixture. Sprinkle with Brazil Nut Parmesan Cheese and garnish with a lemon wedge.

Spinach and Beet Salad

2 servings
. . . .

Ingredients:

2   cups spinach leaves
½   red beet, grated
     Zest and juice of 1 lemon
2   tablespoons raw sesame seeds, toasted
2   tablespoons olive oil
     Brazil Nut Parmesan "Cheese" (optional, see page 81)
     Sea salt and black pepper to taste

Directions: Arrange spinach leaves on 2 plates and top with grated beets. Zest the lemon over each plate, cut the lemon in half, and squeeze over both salads.

Toast the sesame seeds in a skillet over low heat, stirring continuously so they do not burn. Remove from heat when they start to release their aroma.

Drizzle about 1 tablespoon of olive oil over each plate and top with sesame seeds, Brazil Nut Parmesan Cheese, and a sprinkle of sea salt and pepper.

Spring Quinoa Salad

2 servings
. . . .

Ingredients:

1   cup quinoa
2   cups vegetable broth or water
¼   teaspoon sea salt
2   tablespoons olive oil
     Juice of 1 lemon
4   cups spring salad mix
2   carrots, grated or shaved
1   bulb fennel, grated or shaved
½   cup raw walnuts, chopped
     Italian Dressing (see page 77)

Directions: Rinse quinoa in a fine-mesh strainer and place in a small saucepan. Add the vegetable broth or water and ¼ teaspoon of sea salt, and bring to a boil. Reduce heat to low, cover, and simmer for 15 minutes.

Remove from the heat and keep the lid on for another 5 minutes to prevent quinoa from sticking to the bottom of the pan. Fluff with a fork and drizzle with 2 tablespoons olive oil and the juice of 1 lemon. Set aside.

To assemble the salad, place some quinoa on each plate, top with a handful of spring salad mix, and sprinkle with shaved carrot and fennel and a handful of chopped walnuts. Drizzle with Italian Dressing.

WATERCRESS SALAD

2 servings

....

Salad Ingredients:

2   cups watercress, chopped
½   small red or yellow onion, finely chopped
2   red radishes, sliced
1   avocado, sliced
4–5 fresh basil leaves, chiffonade cut
     Fresh ground black pepper to taste

Dressing Ingredients:

2   tablespoons olive oil
     Zest and juice of 1 lemon
⅛   teaspoon sea salt

Directions: Arrange watercress greens on two plates. Top with onion, radishes, avocado slices, and some basil.

In a small bowl or measuring cup, whisk together all of the dressing ingredients and drizzle over the salads. Add fresh ground pepper to taste over each salad.

SHREDDED RAW RAINBOW SALAD

2 servings

....

Ingredients:

1   large carrot, grated
1   large zucchini, grated
1   large yellow squash, grated
¼   cup red onion, thinly sliced
¼   head of red cabbage, grated
¼   cup fresh cilantro, finely chopped
2   scallions, white and green parts thinly sliced
1   cup raw pumpkin seeds
     Juice of 1 lime
2   teaspoons Raw Coconut Aminos
1   tablespoon raw apple cider vinegar
½   teaspoon sea salt

Directions: Place grated carrots, zucchini, yellow squash, and red onion in a large bowl. Peel off the outer layer of the red cabbage and cut it in half and then in half again. Thinly slice ¼ of the head of cabbage and add to bowl. Add chopped cilantro, scallions, and pumpkin seeds, and mix.

In a small bowl or measuring cup, whisk together the lime juice, Coconut Aminos, raw apple cider vinegar, and sea salt. Pour over the shredded vegetable mixture and toss to combine.

Creamy Zucchini-Noodle Salad

2 servings

. . . .

Salad Ingredients:

2	large zucchini, spiralized or grated
½	cup cherry tomatoes, cut in half
¼	cup sliced black olives
4	scallions, white & green parts thinly sliced
¼	cup sun-dried tomatoes in oil, sliced (optional, no need to drain)
¼	cup fresh basil leaves, chiffonade cut

Dressing Ingredients:

	Juice of 1 lemon
¼	cup water
2	tablespoons Raw Coconut Aminos
½	cup raw sesame seeds
¾	cup raw hempseeds
3–4	cloves garlic
1	teaspoon smoked paprika
½	teaspoon sea salt
¼	teaspoon black pepper
¼	teaspoon cayenne pepper (optional)

Directions: Spiralize zucchini to make "noodles" (cut if too long) or grate into long, thin strips. Place in large bowl with other salad ingredients. Place dressing ingredients in blender, adding liquids first. Start with ¼ cup water; add more if too thick. Add seeds, garlic, spices, and salt. Slowly increasing from low to high, blend until creamy. Scrape sides and add more water if needed. Pour dressing over noodles. Stir gently until veggies coated.

Avocado, Hearts of Palm, and Pine Nut Salad

2 servings

. . . .

Ingredients:

1	avocado, cut into bite-sized cubes
½	cup cherry or grape tomatoes, cut in half
1	can/jar hearts of palm, sliced
2	tablespoons olive oil
1	teaspoon raw apple cider vinegar or rice vinegar
	Juice of 1 lemon
¼	teaspoon sea salt
2	tablespoons raw pine nuts, whole, or 8-10 macadamia nuts, chopped

Directions: To make the avocado cubes, cut the avocado in half and remove the pit, and then cut into quarters. Peel and cut into bite-sized cubes. Place in a medium-sized bowl with the tomatoes and hearts of palm.

In a small bowl, mix together the olive oil, rice vinegar, and lemon juice, and drizzle over the avocado and tomatoes. Sprinkle with ¼ teaspoon of sea salt and toss with a spoon. Taste for seasoning.

Top with pine nuts or chopped macadamia nuts before serving.

Marinated Kale Salad

Serves 2

. . . .

Ingredients:

1   bunch black lacinato kale
3   tablespoons olive or avocado oil
    Zest and juice of 1 lemon
1   tablespoon raw apple cider vinegar
½   teaspoon sea salt
¼   teaspoon red pepper flakes (optional)
¼   cup sun-dried tomatoes in oil (optional, no need to drain)
¼   cup raw pumpkin seeds (optional)

Directions: Remove kale stems by holding the end of the stem with one hand and pulling the leaves off towards the top with the other hand. Finely chop the stems into very small pieces, ⅛ of an inch thick or smaller, and place in a large bowl. Chop the leaves into bite-sized pieces and add to the bowl.

In a separate bowl, whisk together the oil, lemon zest and juice, raw apple cider vinegar, sea salt, and red pepper flakes.

Pour the mixture over the kale and, using your hands, massage it into the leaves and stems for about 2–3 minutes. You will start to see and feel the kale getting softer. Toss in the sliced sun-dried tomatoes and pumpkin seeds. Taste for seasoning.

Cucumber-Avocado Salad

4–6 servings

. . . .

Ingredients:

4   Persian cucumbers, unpeeled if organic, diced
1   avocado, diced
½   red onion, small dice
2   tablespoons olive oil
1   tablespoon raw apple cider vinegar
½   teaspoon sea salt
¼   teaspoon black pepper
1   small handful fresh oregano, minced (save small amount for garnish)

Directions: Peel and dice avocado and place in a medium-sized mixing bowl with cucumbers and red onion.

In a separate small bowl or measuring cup, whisk together the olive oil, raw apple cider vinegar, sea salt, and black pepper. Pour over the cucumber mixture and gently stir to combine. Mix in the oregano, reserving a little bit for garnishing when plating.

ALMOND KALE SALAD

Serves 2

* *

Ingredients:

1   bunch kale, rinsed well (keep damp), de-stemmed, and roughly chopped

2–3   tablespoons almond butter

1   tablespoon Raw Coconut Aminos

4–5   drops liquid stevia

2–3   cloves garlic, minced

1   tablespoon water

2   tablespoons slivered almonds for garnish

Directions: In a small bowl, mix together almond butter, Coconut Aminos, stevia, garlic, and water to create a sauce.

To prepare kale, heat a large skillet over high heat. When skillet is nice and hot, add the damp kale. You should hear it start to sizzle. Sauté briefly, for about 1–2 minutes, stirring kale constantly. Add about 1 tablespoon of water and as it starts to steam, quickly cover pan. Keep covered about 1 minute or until kale is evenly cooked.

While kale is still in the hot pan, add the almond butter sauce. Remove from heat and thoroughly mix sauce into the kale. Sprinkle with slivered almonds and serve warm.

SPICY ASIAN COLESLAW

Makes 4 cups

* *

Coleslaw Ingredients:

4   cups shredded green cabbage (or purple, or combination of both)

4   carrots, shredded

½   red onion, very thinly sliced into half moons

5–6   scallions, white and green parts minced

1   teaspoon sea salt

2–4   tablespoons raw sesame seeds

Dressing Ingredients:

¼   cup sesame oil

2   tablespoons hot sauce

2   tablespoons brown rice vinegar

4–5   drops liquid stevia

2   tablespoons Homemade Mayonnaise or Vegan Mayonnaise (see page 74)

    Juice of 2 limes

¼   teaspoon sea salt

¼   teaspoon black pepper

¼   teaspoon red pepper flakes

Directions: In a small bowl, whisk together all of the dressing ingredients and set aside. In a large bowl, place the shredded cabbage, carrots, red onion, and scallions. Sprinkle with 1 teaspoon sea salt and massage with your hands until the vegetables start to break down. This should take about 2–3 minutes. If there is a lot of excess water in the mixture, strain the vegetables. Pour in the dressing and toss to coat evenly. Sprinkle with sesame seeds, and taste for seasoning.

SALMON OR CHICKEN SALAD

2 servings

. . . .

Ingredients:

2   pieces of fresh salmon (⅓ pound each) or 2 large chicken breasts

¼   cup red onion, small dice

1–2 stalks celery, small dice

1   carrot, small dice

1–2 tablespoons fresh dill, chopped

1–2 tablespoons raw walnuts, chopped

½   teaspoon sea salt

¼   teaspoon black pepper

2   tablespoons Homemade Mayonnaise (see page 74)

1   tablespoon mustard

Directions: Preheat oven to 350°F. Bake salmon 10–15 minutes, until you can flake with a fork. If using chicken, sprinkle breasts with pinch of salt and bake 20–30 minutes, until internal temperature is 165°F. While salmon/chicken is cooking, prepare salad ingredients—onion, celery, carrots, dill, walnuts—and mix in a bowl with ¼ teaspoon salt and ¼ teaspoon pepper.

When salmon/chicken is cooked, let cool for 5 minutes. Remove the skin, then flake salmon or break it into small chunks. For chicken, remove the meat from the bone and dice into cubes. Place the chunks of salmon/chicken in the bowl of chopped vegetables, add the mayo and mustard, and mix well. Taste for seasoning. Serve on top of a garden salad, in a lettuce-leaf wrap, on top of avocado halves, or in a warm grain-free wrap (see page 185) or brown-rice tortilla wrap.

CHICKEN CAESAR SALAD

2 servings

. . . .

Salad Ingredients:

8   ounces uncooked boneless chicken breast (more if desired)

1   large head romaine lettuce, cut into bite-sized pieces

1   cup cucumber, chopped

½   cup carrot, shredded

½   sheet of nori seaweed, cut into small strips (optional)

    Almost Sourdough Croutons (optional, see page 186)

Dressing Ingredients:

¼   cup olive oil

    Juice of 1 large or 2 small lemons

¼   cup water, or more, depending on consistency desired

2   heaping tablespoons raw almond butter

3   cloves garlic

1   tablespoon mustard (spicy if desired)

2   tablespoons Raw Coconut Aminos

1   heaping tablespoon raw tahini

¼   teaspoon sea salt

Directions: Preheat oven to 350°F and bake chicken until tender, about 20 minutes. Combine dressing ingredients in a blender, starting with the liquids. Blend until smooth. When chicken is cooked, let cool slightly and then cut into strips. To assemble the salad, toss the lettuce, cucumber, carrots, chicken, and half the nori (save some for garnish) in a serving bowl. Add dressing and toss to combine. Top with croutons and remaining nori strips.

Breads and Snacks

EATING SNACKS DURING THE DAY creates a nice pick-me-up and a change from our usual meal routine. As an additional bonus, eating healthy snacks throughout the day can actually help you lose weight because eating in between meals keeps your metabolism running optimally. One thing that many people miss on a gluten-free diet is the comfort of eating bread, which is why I have included recipes for the wholesome Grain-Free Wrap, Garlic-Rosemary Paleo Bread, and Almost Sourdough Bread or Croutons. To make it easy to add these into your meals, remember that you can make the breads ahead of time and freeze individual slices so they're ready to go when you are.

"Nature cures when given the opportunity."

—BERNARD JENSEN, DC, PHD

Garlic-Rosemary Paleo Bread

6–8 servings

. . . .

Ingredients:

1	cup almond meal
½	cup coconut flour
½	cup ground flaxseeds
1	teaspoon sea salt
½	teaspoon baking soda
1	tablespoon fresh rosemary, minced
6–8	cloves garlic, minced
5	eggs
½	cup olive oil
1	tablespoon raw apple cider vinegar
	Coconut or olive oil spray for loaf pan

Directions: Preheat oven to 350°F. Generously spray a loaf pan with coconut or olive oil spray or coat with 2 tablespoons olive oil.

Remove the needles from the stems of the fresh rosemary and mince to get 1 tablespoon. In a large bowl, whisk together the almond meal, coconut flour, ground flaxseeds, sea salt, baking soda, rosemary, and garlic.

In a separate bowl, whisk together the eggs, ½ cup of olive oil, and raw apple cider vinegar. Pour the wet ingredients into the dry ingredients and stir until everything is well combined.

Pour the batter into the greased loaf pan and bake on the middle rack of the oven for about 40–50 minutes, until bread is firm to the touch and golden brown on top. Let cool for about 5–10 minutes before removing from the loaf pan. Enjoy with organic ghee.

Variation: Add ⅓ cup chopped black and green olives to the batter.

Note: This bread needs to be stored in the refrigerator and will last for about 5–7 days. Or you can pre-slice it and store it in the freezer for up to a month.

Grain-Free Wrap

Makes about 3 wraps

. . . .

Ingredients:

¼   cup arrowroot or tapioca flour
¼   teaspoon baking soda
¼   teaspoon baking powder
¼   teaspoon sea salt
2   eggs
1   teaspoon raw apple cider vinegar
    Coconut or olive oil spray for skillet

Directions: In a small bowl, whisk together arrowroot or tapioca flour, baking soda, baking powder, and salt to remove lumps. In a separate bowl, whisk eggs with the raw apple cider vinegar. Add dry ingredients to egg mixture a little at a time. Whisk vigorously to combine completely.

Heat a nonstick skillet over medium heat and spray generously with coconut or olive oil spray. When hot, spoon ¼ cup of batter onto skillet, spreading it into a circle. Pick up the skillet and slightly rotate it around in a circle to help distribute the batter. Let cook for 1 minute, then flip with a spatula and cook other side for about 30 seconds more.

Remove wrap from heat and let cool on a cooling rack. Enjoy with pasture butter, almond butter, or fresh mashed apple. Or use with any of the Main Dish recipes that call for a wrap.

Variation: For a sweet wrap, mix in 1 teaspoon vanilla extract, 1 teaspoon cinnamon, and 1 teaspoon xylitol (or 2 drops liquid stevia) with the wet or dry ingredients.

Almost Sourdough Bread

6-8 servings

. . . .

Ingredients:

1¼   cups brown rice flour
1   cup tapioca flour
½   cup sesame seeds
2   tablespoons whole caraway seeds
     (omit if using for French toast)
½   teaspoon sea salt
2   eggs
2   tablespoons olive oil
½   cup coconut or almond milk
½   cup water
¼   cup raw apple cider vinegar
1   teaspoon baking soda
1   teaspoon baking powder
2   tablespoons flaxseed meal
     Coconut or olive oil spray to grease pan

Directions: Preheat oven to 350°F. Spray pan with oil. In a large bowl, whisk together brown rice flour, tapioca flour, sesame and caraway seeds, flaxseed meal, and salt. In a separate bowl, whisk eggs, oil, nondairy milk, water, vinegar, baking soda, and baking powder. Mix wet ingredients into dry until well combined. Pour batter into greased loaf pan and bake on middle rack of oven for 50 minutes or until bread is firm to the touch and golden brown on top. Let cool for 5–10 minutes before removing from pan. Cool on a cooling rack before slicing. Enjoy with organic butter or ghee or use for sandwiches. Store in refrigerator for 5–7 days, or pre-slice and freeze for a month or more.

ALMOST SOURDOUGH CROUTONS

2 servings

....

Ingredients:

4   slices Almost Sourdough Bread, cut into ½-inch cubes (see page 185)
2   teaspoons dried oregano
2   teaspoons dried basil
1   teaspoon garlic powder
½   teaspoon sea salt
¼   cup olive oil, divided

Directions: Preheat oven to 350°F and grease a baking sheet with 2 tablespoons of olive oil.

In a medium-sized bowl, mix the spices, sea salt, and remaining olive oil. Add the bread cubes and use your hands to evenly coat them with the oil mixture.

Spread the croutons onto the oiled baking sheet and bake for 15 minutes or until golden brown. Stir them halfway through the baking time to make sure they brown evenly.

BAKED KABOCHA SQUASH SLICES

2–3 servings

....

Ingredients:

1   kabocha squash, sliced into ⅛–¼-inch wedges
¼   cup grapeseed oil
¼   teaspoon sea salt
½   teaspoon cinnamon (optional)
¼   teaspoon ground ginger (optional)
    Coconut or olive oil spray for baking sheet

Directions: Preheat oven to 400°F. Generously spray a baking sheet with coconut or olive oil spray. Cut washed squash in half lengthwise, remove the seeds, and slice each half into ⅛–¼-inch wedges. Place in a medium-sized mixing bowl.

In a small bowl or measuring cup, mix together the ¼ cup grapeseed oil, sea salt, and spices of your choice and pour over the squash, coating the pieces well.

Place the squash on the baking sheet and bake for 10 minutes. Remove from the oven and flip the slices over with a spatula. Continue baking for another 5 minutes or until desired crispness is reached.

Quinoa Cakes

2–4 servings

....

Ingredients:

¾   cup uncooked quinoa or 1 cup cooked
    quinoa

1½ cups water or vegetable broth to cook
    quinoa

1   cup raw sweet potato, cut into small cubes

¼   red pepper, small dice

¼   zucchini, small dice

¼   cup red onion, small dice

3   tablespoons tapioca flour

1   egg, beaten

½   teaspoon sea salt, plus few pinches

1   teaspoon fresh thyme, minced

½   teaspoon chili pepper flakes (optional)

¼   cup grapeseed oil for frying patties, plus 2
    tablespoons, divided, for sautéing

Directions: Rinse ¾ cup quinoa and place
in a small saucepan with 1½ cups water or
vegetable broth and a pinch of sea salt. Bring
to a boil over high heat, reduce to low, cover,
and simmer for 15 minutes. When liquid is
absorbed, remove the pan from the heat, but
keep the lid on for another 5 minutes to prevent
quinoa from sticking to the bottom of the pan.
Set aside.

Heat 1 tablespoon grapeseed oil in a medium-
sized skillet and sauté cubed sweet potato over
medium-high heat until soft. Transfer sweet

potato to a mixing bowl and mash with a fork or
potato masher.

In the same skillet, heat 1 tablespoon of
grapeseed oil and a pinch of sea salt and sauté
the red pepper, zucchini, and red onion over
medium heat, stirring continuously for 3–4
minutes or until the vegetables start to soften.
Set aside.

Place the cooked quinoa in a food processor
and add the sautéed vegetables, tapioca flour,
beaten egg, ½ teaspoon sea salt, thyme, and
chili pepper flakes. Pulse a couple of times to
combine. Remove from the food processor and
place in a large mixing bowl.

Form the mixture into small patties. Heat ¼ cup
grapeseed oil in a large skillet over medium
heat, and when oil is hot, pan-fry each patty for
about 3–4 minutes on each side.

Enjoy over a mixed green salad.

CRISPY BAKED KALE CHIPS

1–2 servings

. . . .

Ingredients:

1   bunch kale
1   tablespoon coconut oil or grapeseed oil
1   teaspoon sea salt
½   teaspoon dried oregano, thyme, or basil
¼   teaspoon red pepper flakes (optional)

Directions: Preheat the oven to 400°F. Line a baking sheet with parchment paper.

With a knife, carefully remove the leaves of the kale from the stems and cut into bite-sized pieces. Wash and thoroughly dry the kale in a salad spinner or with a towel.

Place the kale into a mixing bowl, and add oil, sea salt, herbs, and red pepper flakes. Massage all of the ingredients into the kale with your hands.

Place the kale on the baking sheet and bake until the edges brown but do not burn, about 10–15 minutes.

SAVORY OR SWEET NUT MIX

3–5 servings

. . . .

Savory Ingredients:

1½   cups raw nuts (almonds, pecans, walnuts), roughly chopped
1   tablespoon fresh rosemary, minced
3   sprigs fresh thyme, minced
¼   teaspoon sea salt
½   teaspoon cumin seeds or ground cumin
½   teaspoon dried garlic (powder or flakes)
1   egg white, beaten
1   tablespoon butter, melted

Sweet Ingredients:

1½   cups raw nuts (almonds, pecans, walnuts), roughly chopped
¼   cup xylitol or 20 drops liquid stevia
2   teaspoons cinnamon
1   egg white, beaten
1   tablespoon butter, melted
¼   teaspoon sea salt

Directions: Preheat oven to 300°F and line a baking sheet with parchment paper. Place nuts in a medium-sized mixing bowl. For savory mix, add fresh and dried spices and sea salt. For sweet mix, add xylitol or stevia, cinnamon, and sea salt. For both, stir in the beaten egg white and melted butter.

Pour coated nuts onto the baking sheet and bake for about 45 minutes. Halfway through the baking time, remove from oven and stir so that the mix gets evenly baked.

ARAME WITH CARROTS AND ONIONS

4–5 servings

. . . .

Ingredients:

1   ounce arame (about one large handful)
Purified water for soaking

1–2 teaspoons toasted sesame oil

½   cup onion, sliced into half moons
Pinch of sea salt

½   cup carrot, cut into fine matchsticks

2   inches of burdock root, peeled and sliced into fine matchsticks

¼   cup Raw Coconut Aminos

1   scallion, white and green parts thinly sliced

2   tablespoons sesame seeds

Directions: Arame needs to be soaked before it is used. Place it in a bowl, cover it with purified water, and soak for 5 minutes. Lift arame out of soaking water with a fork or slotted spoon, leaving any grit behind. Cut any long strands of arame into 2-inch pieces.

Heat the sesame oil in a medium skillet over medium-high heat. Add the onion and a tiny pinch of sea salt. Sauté for 1–2 minutes.

Add the carrot and burdock to the skillet and sauté for a couple of minutes more. Sprinkle arame on top.

Without stirring, add Coconut Aminos and enough water to cover only the vegetables, leaving the arame just above the water.

Bring to a boil, reduce heat to low, and cover the skillet. Simmer for 25–30 minutes. Check occasionally to make sure the water has not completely cooked off. If it has, add a little more. When done, the water should be completely cooked off.

Garnish with scallions and sesame seeds, and serve warm or cold.

Vegetable Nori Rolls

Makes 3–4 rolls

. . . .

Ingredients:

1	cup uncooked brown rice
2	cups water
	Pinch of sea salt
1	carrot, thinly sliced into matchsticks
1	cucumber, thinly sliced, into matchsticks
1	avocado, thinly sliced
1	cup fresh arugula, cut into small pieces
½	cup homemade horseradish sauce (see page 91)
¼	cup toasted sesame seeds, black or golden
2–3	sheets nori
	Bamboo sushi mat
	1 medium-sized bowl of water to keep fingers moist

Dipping Sauce:

2	tablespoons Raw Coconut Aminos
1	teaspoon sesame oil
	Juice of ½ lime

Directions: Rinse the rice in a fine-mesh strainer under cold running water, swirling the rice around with your hand, until the water runs clear. Place rice in a medium-sized saucepan with 2 cups of water and a pinch of sea salt. Bring to a boil, reduce heat to low, cover, and let simmer for 40 minutes. Remove from heat and let it sit for about 5 minutes before removing the lid to prevent rice from sticking to the bottom of the pan.

While the rice is cooking, cut the carrots, cucumber, avocado, and arugula, keeping each vegetable separate. Set aside. Make the horseradish if you have not already prepared it, and set aside. To toast sesame seeds, place in a small skillet over low heat and stir continuously for 3–5 minutes. Remove from burner when seeds begin to release their aroma.

When the rice is finished cooking and has cooled slightly, you are ready to start. Place one sheet of nori, shiny side down, on the bamboo sushi mat. Moisten your fingers and spread about ⅓ cup of cooked rice to evenly cover the bottom ¾ of the nori sheet with a ¼-inch-thick layer of rice. Press the rice all the way out to the sides and lower edge of the sheet. Do not put any rice on the top ½ inch of the nori sheet. Lightly sprinkle the sesame seeds over the rice. In about the center of the layer of rice, place a row of the carrot, cucumber, avocado, horseradish, and arugula.

Gently but firmly, roll the nori from the bottom, using the mat to help make a tight roll. When you reach the ½-inch edge of nori, lightly moisten it with water, fold over, and press to seal the roll. Continue making rolls with the remaining ingredients. Using a wet serrated knife, slice the rolls into 1-inch-thick slices. epare the dipping sauce by simply whisking together the sauce ingredients.

Beverages

WATER MAKES UP 70 percent of your body's fluid mass, so it stands to reason that staying hydrated each day is essential for your health. The easiest way to stay hydrated is to drink six ounces of purified water every waking hour. Tea counts as water, but since many teas have diuretic properties, it's important to drink water as well. For variety—and an easy way to take in more minerals, vitamins, and antioxidants—enjoy the teas, dairy-free milks, juices, smoothies, and delicious hot beverages in this section.

"The natural healing force within each one of us is the greatest force in getting well. Our food should be our medicine. Our medicine should be our food."

—HIPPOCRATES

Brazil Nut Milk

Makes 3–4 cups

....

Ingredients:

2   cups raw Brazil nuts (soaked for 4 hours)
¼   teaspoon sea salt
¼   teaspoon cinnamon
1   teaspoon vanilla extract
4   cups purified water
4–6 drops liquid stevia (optional)

Directions: After the Brazil nuts have been soaked for 4 hours, discard soaking water and rinse the nuts in a fine-mesh strainer.

Place nuts into a Vitamix or high-powered blender and add sea salt, cinnamon, vanilla, 4 cups water, and stevia. Start blending on low speed, gradually increasing to high, until it reaches a creamy consistency.

Using a nut milk bag, cheesecloth, or an extremely fine-mesh strainer, strain the pulp out of the milk and discard.

Store milk in a glass jar in the refrigerator for up to 3–5 days.

Almond Milk

Makes 3–4 cups

....

Ingredients:

1   cup blanched almonds (purchase or blanch yourself)
4   cups purified water (less or more for desired consistency)
⅛   teaspoon sea salt
1   teaspoon vanilla extract (optional)
5+   drops liquid stevia (optional)

Directions: Blend all ingredients well in blender. Pour into a glass jar and refrigerate. Will store for up to 6 days.

Hot Yerba Maté Latte

Makes 1 large cup

. . . .

Ingredients:

1   tablespoon yerba maté powder
1½ cups water
½   cup almond or hemp milk
1   teaspoon coconut oil
¼   teaspoon cinnamon
    Couple drops liquid stevia (optional)

Directions: Bring 1½ cups of water to a boil. Meanwhile, place the almond or hemp milk, coconut oil, yerba maté powder, and cinnamon in a blender. Add boiled water to blender.

Place a dish towel over the lid to protect your hand, and start blending at a low speed, gradually increasing to high. Blend for about 30–45 seconds or until mixture starts to look frothy. Pour into your favorite coffee mug.

Note: If you would like a stronger latte, add more yerba maté, 1 teaspoon at a time. Wisdom of the Ancients Instant Yerba Mate Royale is sweetened with stevia, so there is no need to add additional sweetener when using this brand.

Cardamom Chai

Makes 2–3 cups

. . . .

Ingredients:

2   cups purified water
1   cup almond or hemp milk
1   ½- inch piece fresh ginger, peeled and thinly sliced
2   star anises
⅛   teaspoon ground cardamom
¼   teaspoon cinnamon
½   teaspoon ground nutmeg
4   dandelion tea bags
1   tablespoon xylitol
10 drops liquid stevia

Note: For those who are xylitol sensitive, use a total of about 15–16 drops of liquid stevia instead of xylitol. Stevia amounts need to be adjusted based on personal taste.

Directions: In a medium-sized saucepan, add the water and nondairy milk.

Wash and peel the fresh ginger and thinly slice. Add the ginger, star anises, cardamom, cinnamon, and nutmeg to the saucepan. Bring the liquid to a boil, cover, and reduce heat to medium-low. Let simmer for about 5–10 minutes.

Turn off the heat and stir in xylitol and stevia. Add the 4 dandelion tea bags, cover, and let steep for another 5 minutes. Strain the liquid to remove the whole spices and tea bags.

DANDELION-GINGER TWIST

Makes 6 cups

. . . .

Ingredients:

4   dandelion tea bags
⅓   cup fresh ginger, peeled and chopped
6   cups purified water
     Juice of 1–2 lemons
10   drops liquid stevia

Directions: In a large saucepan, bring the water to a boil. Remove from the heat, add the tea bags and chopped ginger. Cover with a tight-fitting lid, and let steep for about 10–15 minutes.

Add lemon juice and stevia to taste. Pour into a large tea pitcher or in mason jars with lids and chill in the refrigerator.

LAVENDER LEMONADE

Makes 4 cups

. . . .

Ingredients:

4   cups purified water
10   drops liquid stevia or ¼ cup xylitol
     Juice of 2 lemons
¼   teaspoon fresh lavender, minced (optional)

Directions: Place all of the ingredients into a glass container and mix well. Serve over ice, if desired.

Mexican Hot Chocolate

Makes 2 cups

. . . .

Ingredients:

1   cup almond milk
1   cup coconut milk
2   tablespoons cocoa powder (unsweetened)
¼   teaspoon Chinese 5 spice
¼   teaspoon sea salt
¼   teaspoon cayenne pepper
1   tablespoon xylitol plus 10 drops liquid stevia

Directions: Starting with the liquids first, place all of the ingredients into a blender. Blend for a few seconds until thoroughly combined.

Pour the mixture into a medium-sized saucepan and heat over medium heat, stirring continuously for about 5 minutes or until the liquid has reached the desired temperature. Experiment with the ratio of sweeteners to find your desired sweetness.

Lemon-Vanilla Ginger Ale

Makes 3–4 cups

. . . .

Ingredients:

¾   cup fresh ginger, peeled and chopped
3½   cups water
2   tablespoons vanilla extract
1   tablespoon lemon extract
15   drops liquid stevia
      Sparkling mineral water (unsweetened)

Directions: In a medium-sized saucepan, add water and ginger. Rapidly boil for ten minutes.

Strain into a large enough jar to hold the concentrate. Stir in the vanilla and lemon extracts and stevia. Cool before storing in the refrigerator.

To serve, add sparkling mineral water to your desired concentration.

Vegetable Alkalizer Juice

1 serving

....

Ingredients:

3	stalks celery
½	small carrot
½	green apple
½	cucumber
4–5	large handfuls of raw spinach, watercress, chard, dark-green lettuces, kale, dandelion greens, cilantro and/or parsley (mix and vary)
1	small clove peeled garlic (optional)
1	1-inch piece fresh ginger (optional)
1	1-inch piece fresh turmeric (optional)

Directions: Run ingredients through a vegetable juice extractor (Breville preferred).

Drink juice immediately on an empty stomach, either an hour before a meal or 2–3 hours after a meal.

Hibiscus Mint Tea

Makes 6 cups

....

Ingredients:

4	hibiscus tea bags
½	cup fresh mint leaves
6	cups purified water
	Juice of 1–2 limes
10	drops liquid stevia

Directions: In a large saucepan, bring the water to a boil. Remove from heat and add tea bags and mint leaves. Cover with a tight-fitting lid and let steep for 10–15 minutes.

Add lime juice and stevia to taste. Pour into a large tea pitcher or in mason jars with lids and chill in the refrigerator.

GREEN PROTEIN POWER SMOOTHIE

1 large serving

. . . .

Ingredients:

1	cup water or nondairy milk
1	serving protein powder (egg, hemp, or rice)
1	cup (packed) spinach leaves
2	tablespoons flaxseeds
¼	teaspoon spirulina, chlorella powder, or 1 scoop of NanoGreens
¼	teaspoon cinnamon
¼	small avocado (optional)
1	tablespoon almond butter
½	cup ice cubes
¼	cup fresh berries
5–6	drops liquid stevia

Directions: Put all of the ingredients into a high-powered blender or NutriBullet, starting with the liquid, and blend until smooth and creamy.

STRAWBERRIES 'N' CREAM PROTEIN SMOOTHIE

1 serving

. . . .

Ingredients:

1	cup coconut milk
2	cups strawberries, frozen or fresh
1	serving protein powder (egg, hemp, or rice)
2	tablespoons flaxseeds or flaxseed meal
½–1	cup ice cubes

Directions: Put all of the ingredients into a high-powered blender or NutriBullet, starting with the coconut milk, and blend until smooth and creamy.

Desserts

WHO DOESN'T LOVE DESSERT? When people think of an anti-candida diet, they think, "I can't have desserts." I'm here to brighten your day and say, "Yes, you can!" The desserts in this section are scrumptious and use only ingredients that are safe for those on the candida-cure diet. I do suggest limiting desserts to three times a week because eating too much xylitol, brown rice flour, or almond butter will increase your carbohydrate intake and feed candida. If you are xylitol-sensitive, try substituting stevia, chicory root, or lo han. You'll find some suggested conversion ratios on page 32, but experiment with the amounts to get the taste you like. Go ahead and savor these guilt-free goodies!

"Satisfy your sweet tooth naturally with fresh fruit or desserts made with natural ingredients…. A treat doesn't have to be sweet. Sometimes it just has to be something new and different."

—ANN LOUISE GITTLEMAN, PHD, CNS

LEMON BARS

12 servings

. . . .

Crust Ingredients:

- ¾ cup brown rice flour or almond meal flour
- ¼ cup tapioca flour
- ⅓ cup Just Like Sugar—Table Top (chicory root)
- ½ teaspoon xanthan gum
- ½ teaspoon sea salt (if your butter is salted, omit this)
- 1 stick unsalted butter, cold and cut into small cubes
- 2–4 tablespoons water
    Coconut oil spray for baking dish

Filling Ingredients:

- ¼ cup xylitol
- ½ cup Just Like Sugar—Table Top
- 2 dropperfuls liquid stevia (about 40 drops)
    Zest of 2 lemons
- ½ cup fresh lemon juice
- 3 tablespoons tapioca flour
- 2 large eggs
- ¼ teaspoon sea salt

Crust Directions: Preheat oven to 350ºF and have one of the racks in the middle position. Spray an 8 x 8-inch baking dish with coconut oil spray.

Place the dry ingredients for the crust in a food processor. Pulse to combine. Cut the butter into small cubes and add to the food processor. Pulse again until no large pieces of butter remain. While the processor is still running, add water, starting with 2 tablespoons, and adding more just until all the dough comes together.

Remove dough from the food processor and place into prepared baking dish. With damp hands, spread the dough evenly along the bottom of the dish. Bake for about 35–40 minutes, until it is golden brown.

Filling Directions: Place all of the filling ingredients in a medium-sized mixing bowl and whisk until fully combined.

When the crust has finished baking, remove from the oven and pour the filling over it. Return to the oven and continue baking for another 20–25 minutes or until the filling is set and does not jiggle.

Remove from the oven and place on a wire rack to cool. Chill bars in the refrigerator for about 2 hours before cutting.

Gluten-Free Zucchini or Carrot Muffins

Makes 12 muffins

....

Ingredients:

1½   cups shredded zucchini or carrot

1   tablespoon chia seeds

¾   cup water

2   teaspoons raw apple cider vinegar

2   tablespoons grapeseed oil

1   teaspoon vanilla extract

1   tablespoon fresh lemon juice

¾   cup almond meal

1   cup sweet sorghum flour

1   teaspoon baking soda

1   teaspoon baking powder

¼   teaspoon sea salt

½   cup xylitol

1   teaspoon cinnamon

½   cup raw walnuts, chopped

      Silicone muffin tin or muffin tin liners

      Coconut or olive oil spray for muffin tin

Directions: Preheat oven to 350°F. Grease muffin tin with coconut or olive oil spray, or use muffin tin liners. Shred the zucchini or carrots with a box grater, place in a small bowl, and set aside.

Place the chia seeds, water, raw apple cider vinegar, grapeseed oil, vanilla, and lemon juice in a blender and let sit for about 5 minutes so that the chia seeds plump up.

In a large bowl, place the almond meal, the sorghum flour, baking soda, baking powder, sea salt, xylitol, and cinnamon, and whisk well to evenly combine.

After the chia seed mixture has been in the blender for 5 minutes, blend for 1–2 minutes. Pour mixture into the bowl of dry ingredients and mix well. Stir in the shredded zucchini or carrots and the chopped walnuts.

Using a spoon or an ice cream scoop, drop the batter into the muffin tin or liners, filling them ¾ full. Tap muffin tin gently on the counter to pop any air bubbles. Bake for about 25 minutes (15–20 minutes if you are using a mini muffin tin).

After removing from the oven, let cool in the pan for about 5 minutes. Carefully remove muffins from the tin and let them continue to cool on a cooling rack.

Grain-Free and Nut-Free Pumpkin Cookies

Makes 12 cookies

. . . .

Ingredients:

¾   cup pumpkin puree (canned)
½   cup coconut oil (melted) or sunflower oil
6   eggs
2   teaspoons vanilla
¼   cup xylitol
½   cup coconut flour
1   teaspoon cinnamon
1   teaspoon nutmeg
1   teaspoon allspice
½   teaspoon baking powder
1   cup shredded coconut
       Coconut oil spray for baking sheet

Directions: Preheat oven to 375°F. Line a baking sheet with parchment paper and spray it with coconut oil spray.

If using coconut oil for the cookies, melt ½ cup in a small saucepan over low heat. Place the pumpkin puree, melted coconut oil or sunflower oil, eggs, vanilla, and xylitol in a blender or large mixing bowl and blend or mix well.

In a small bowl, sift together the coconut flour, cinnamon, nutmeg, allspice, and baking powder. Add that to the pumpkin mixture, stirring until all the lumps are gone. Add the shredded coconut and mix well.

Scoop heaping tablespoonfuls of batter onto the baking sheet (do not flatten) and bake for about 10–12 minutes or until the bottoms start to turn golden brown.

Remove the baking sheet from the oven, let the cookies cool for about 2 minutes, and then transfer to a cooling rack to cool completely.

Store in an airtight container in the refrigerator for up to 1 week.

GINGER-SPICED COOKIES

Makes 9 large or 12 small cookies

. . . .

Ingredients:

½	cup almond butter or tahini butter (or ¼ cup of each)
½	cup shredded coconut
¼	cup xylitol
¼	teaspoon sea salt
1	teaspoon ginger powder
1	teaspoon ground cinnamon
1	egg
	Coconut oil spray for baking sheet

Directions: Preheat oven to 350°F. Line a baking sheet with parchment paper and spray with coconut oil spray.

Place all of the ingredients in a food processor and blend until fully combined.

Place 1–2 tablespoons of batter at a time onto the baking sheet, depending on size of cookie you are making. Press batter down with a fork to flatten and bake for 15–18 minutes or until the cookies turn golden brown. Let cool on a cooling rack. Store in the refrigerator.

Note: If you prefer sweeter cookies, add ¼ teaspoon of stevia powder or 6 drops of liquid stevia when blending batter.

ALMOND BUTTER AND CHOCOLATE CHEWS

10–12 servings

. . . .

Ingredients:

½	cup almond butter
½	teaspoon ground cinnamon
1	teaspoon vanilla
2	tablespoons shredded coconut, plus more for rolling (optional)
2	tablespoons xylitol or 10 drops liquid stevia
1	cup puffed millet or rice (brown)
¼	cup stevia-sweetened chocolate chips (only Lily's brand is acceptable for this recipe)

Directions: In a medium-sized bowl, stir together the almond butter, cinnamon, vanilla, shredded coconut, and xylitol or stevia. Gently mix in the puffed millet or rice and chocolate chips.

Dampen your hands and roll 1–2 tablespoons of the mixture at a time into small balls between your palms, gently squeezing to pack them together.

Place in a container in a single layer, and let firm in the refrigerator for about 1 hour. Store in the refrigerator in an airtight container.

Note: It's important to make sure that the almond butter you use is not dry, or the chews will not hold together. When you open a new jar, make sure to stir well to mix all the oil in with the almond butter.

Baked Apple, Berry, or Berry-Rhubarb Crumble

6–8 servings

. . . .

Fruit Mixture Ingredients:

3–4   green apples, ¼-inch slices; or 3–4 cups mixed fresh berries; or 2½ cups mixed fresh berries plus 1½ cups rhubarb, cut into ½-inch cubes
2   tablespoons xylitol
20   drops liquid stevia
1   heaping tablespoon arrowroot
1   teaspoon ground cinnamon (only for apple crumble)
¼   cup water
       Juice of 1 lemon
1   tablespoon vanilla extract
¼   teaspoon sea salt
       Coconut oil spray for pie dish

Crumble Ingredients:

1   cup quick-cooking gluten-free oats
½   cup raw sunflower seeds or slivered almonds
¼   cup coconut flour
¼   cup almond meal
¼   cup xylitol
½   teaspoon baking powder
¼   teaspoon baking soda
¼   teaspoon sea salt
½   cup melted butter

Fruit Mixture Directions: Preheat oven to 350°F and spray a pie dish with coconut oil spray.

Slice the apples or cut up any large berries and chop the rhubarb stalks if using. Place fruit in oiled pie dish.

In a small bowl, whisk together the xylitol, stevia, arrowroot, cinnamon (omit cinnamon for mixed berry and berry/rhubarb recipes), water, lemon juice, vanilla, and sea salt. Pour over the fruit.

Crumble Directions: In a separate bowl, combine the oats, sunflower seeds (or almonds), coconut flour, almond meal, xylitol, baking powder, baking soda, and sea salt. In a small saucepan, melt the butter, pour it over this mixture, and stir to coat. Sprinkle crumble mixture evenly over the fruit.

Cover pie dish with foil and bake for about 30–35 minutes or until the apples and/or rhubarb are tender. Remove the foil for the last 5–10 minutes of baking to brown the crumble. Serve warm.

Chocolate Quinoa Cupcakes with Chocolate Coconut-Cream Frosting

Makes 12 cupcakes

. . . .

Cupcake Ingredients:

1	cup uncooked white quinoa or 2 cups cooked quinoa
2	cups water for cooking quinoa
²⁄₃	cup almond milk
4	eggs
2	teaspoons vanilla extract
¾	cup coconut oil
3	tablespoons xylitol
20	drops liquid stevia
1	cup unsweetened cocoa powder
1½	teaspoons baking powder
½	teaspoon baking soda
½	teaspoon sea salt
	Silicone 12-cupcake tin or cupcake liners
	Coconut oil spray for cupcake tin

Frosting Ingredients:

½	cup firm coconut cream*
½	ripe avocado
⅓	cup cocoa powder
1	teaspoon vanilla extract
15	drops liquid stevia (more if desired)
1½	tablespoons xylitol
	Pinch of sea salt

Directions: Preheat oven to 350°F. Spray cupcake tin with coconut oil spray or place liners in a 12-cupcake tin.

To cook the quinoa, rinse it well and place in a small saucepan with 2 cups of water and a pinch of sea salt. Bring to a boil, reduce heat to low, and simmer for about 15–20 minutes or until all the liquid has been absorbed. Remove from burner and let cool for about 5 minutes with the lid on.

Place cooked quinoa and the rest of the cupcake ingredients in a blender. Starting on low speed and gradually increasing to high, blend for about 3–5 minutes or until the mixture is nice and smooth. The consistency will not be thick. Scoop mixture into the cupcake tin and bake for 20–25 minutes or until a toothpick comes out clean. After removing from the oven, let sit in the cupcake tin for about 5 minutes. Carefully remove cupcakes from the pan and let them continue to cool on a cooling rack.

To make the frosting, first place ½ cup of firm coconut cream into a blender and then add the rest of the frosting ingredients. Blend until smooth and creamy. Taste for sweetness, and if you prefer it sweeter, add a couple more drops of stevia or a little more xylitol. Put in the refrigerator so that the frosting sets.

*Coconut cream is generally firm but may get runny if the temperature is warm. The cream must be firm to make this frosting properly, so if it's not, place in refrigerator for about 1–2 hours to firm it up.

Coconut Muffins

Makes 8 large muffins

....

Ingredients:

2   cups shredded coconut, ground

¼   cup (packed) almond flour

1   tablespoon sifted coconut flour

⅓   cup xylitol

⅛   teaspoon sea salt

½   teaspoon baking powder

2   tablespoons coconut oil, melted

3   large eggs

2   teaspoons vanilla extract or coconut extract

¼   cup coconut milk

     Silicone muffin tin or muffin tin liners

     Coconut or olive oil spray for muffin tin

Directions: Preheat oven to 325°F and spray muffin tin with oil. In a food processor or NutriBullet, grind shredded coconut into a fine, powdery meal. Pack almond flour into a ¼-cup measuring cup and sweep level. In a small bowl, mix coconut meal, almond flour, coconut flour, xylitol, sea salt, and baking powder. If coconut oil is solid, melt in a saucepan over low heat and then transfer to large mixing bowl. Beat in eggs, vanilla or coconut extract, and coconut milk. Add the dry ingredients and beat for 2 minutes.

Pour batter into the muffin tin or liners, filling them ¾ full. Tap muffin tin gently on counter to pop any air bubbles. Bake about 25–30 minutes or until muffins are springy and firm to the touch. Remove from tin as soon as they're cool to the touch. Continue cooling on a wire rack and serve at room temperature. Refrigerate leftovers.

Paleo Fudgy Brownies

Makes 12 brownies

....

Ingredients:

¼   cup plain or vanilla almond milk

2   eggs

1   teaspoon vanilla extract

⅓   cup cocoa powder (unsweetened)

¼   teaspoon baking soda

⅛   teaspoon sea salt

½   cup almond butter, creamy or crunchy

½   cup xylitol

⅓   cup coconut oil

     Coconut oil spray for baking pan

Directions: Preheat oven to 325°F and grease an 8 x 8-inch pan with coconut oil spray. Place all of the ingredients into a blender, starting with the liquid, and blend until smooth, scraping down the sides if necessary.

Pour into pan and bake for 40–45 minutes or until a toothpick comes out clean.

Chocolaty Avocado Pudding

4 servings

. . . .

Ingredients:

2	ripe avocados
¼	cup coconut cream
¼	cup cocoa powder
2	tablespoons carob powder
1	teaspoon vanilla
¼	cup xylitol or 20 drops liquid stevia, depending on preference
¼	cup applesauce
¼	cup nondairy milk
⅛	teaspoon sea salt
	Slivered almonds for garnish (optional)
	Shredded coconut for garnish (optional)
	Handful of blueberries for garnish (optional)

Directions: Put all the ingredients (except almonds, coconut, or blueberries) in a food processor and blend until smooth and creamy, scraping down the sides occasionally. Garnish with slivered almonds and a sprinkle of shredded coconut.

Note: If the avocados are not quite ripe enough, you may need to add up to ¼ cup more of nondairy milk when blending.

Paleo Cacao Chip Cookies

Makes 8–12 cookies

. . . .

Ingredients:

1	cup almond flour
1	tablespoon shredded coconut
¼	teaspoon sea salt
½	tablespoon vanilla extract
¼	cup coconut oil
¼	cup xylitol
2	tablespoons water
⅓	cup cacao nibs
	Coconut oil spray for baking sheet

Directions: Preheat oven to 350ºF. Line baking sheet with parchment paper and spray with coconut oil spray. In medium-sized bowl, whisk together almond flour, shredded coconut, and sea salt, removing lumps. In a small saucepan, mix vanilla, coconut oil, xylitol, and water. Bring to a low simmer. This will help dissolve the xylitol. Pour mixture into bowl of dry ingredients and mix thoroughly. Stir in cacao nibs.

Using a mini ice cream scoop or tablespoon, scoop 1 tablespoon at a time onto prepared baking sheet, leaving about 1 inch between each spoonful of batter. After all of the batter is placed on the pan, flatten each one slightly with the palm of your hand. Bake for 8–10 minutes or until edges just start to turn brown. Remove baking sheet from oven and let sit for 1 minute. Remove cookies using a spatula, and place on a cooling rack to cool completely. Store in airtight container in refrigerator for longest shelf life.

Pumpkin Pudding

3–4 servings

....

Ingredients:

1   (15-ounce) can pumpkin puree

2   tablespoons arrowroot flour

1   cup full-fat coconut milk or other nondairy milk

1   teaspoon vanilla extract

¼   cup xylitol or 20 drops liquid stevia

1   teaspoon pumpkin pie spice

¼   cup raw nuts (pecans, slivered almonds, macadamia nuts), chopped

Directions: In a small bowl, dissolve the arrowroot in the milk, breaking up any lumps. Set aside.

In a medium saucepan, place the pumpkin, vanilla, xylitol or stevia, and pumpkin pie spice, and heat over medium heat. Stir in the arrowroot and milk mixture and whisk together for about 5 minutes, until you notice the mixture start to thicken. If it does not get thick enough, add a little more dissolved arrowroot.

When the pudding reaches your desired consistency, place in small glass cups or dishes and garnish with chopped nuts. Place in the refrigerator to set.

Apple-Almond Butter Sandwiches

2–4 servings

....

Ingredients:

2   Granny Smith apples, cored and cut lengthwise into ½-inch slices

¼   cup almond butter

¼   teaspoon almond extract

¼   teaspoon vanilla extract

½   teaspoon cinnamon

¼   teaspoon sea salt (omit if your almond butter has sea salt)

5   drops liquid stevia

¼   cup shredded coconut

     Juice of 1 lemon

1   tablespoon water, if needed

Directions: Remove the core of the apples with an apple corer and cut the apples horizontally into ½-inch slices. Squeeze the juice of 1 lemon over the apple slices to prevent browning.

In a small bowl, mix together the almond butter, almond extract, vanilla extract, cinnamon, sea salt, and stevia. If the mixture is too thick, stir in about 1 tablespoon of water to loosen it up slightly.

Spread the almond butter mixture onto one side of an apple slice, sprinkle coconut on top, and place a plain apple slice on top of it to make a sandwich. Continue until all of the slices are used. Cut "sandwiches" in half if you like before serving. If you do not eat all of them immediately, store in the refrigerator in an airtight container.

CHOCOLATE HAZELNUT BISCOTTI

8–10 servings

. . . .

Ingredients:

¾   cup almond meal
¼   cup tapioca starch
¼   cup coconut flour
½   cup xylitol
¼   cup cocoa powder
¼   teaspoon sea salt
½   teaspoon baking soda
⅓   cup hazelnuts, chopped
½   cup cacao nibs
1   egg
1½ tablespoons vanilla extract
3   tablespoons coconut or grapeseed oil
       Coconut oil spray for baking sheet

Directions: Preheat oven to 350°F. Line baking sheet with parchment paper and spray with oil. In a large mixing bowl, whisk almond meal, tapioca starch, coconut flour, xylitol, cocoa powder, sea salt, and baking soda to combine well and remove lumps. Stir in chopped hazelnuts and cacao nibs. In a separate bowl, whisk egg, vanilla, and oil. If using coconut oil, liquefy by heating briefly in a saucepan over low heat. Add wet mixture to the dry and stir well.

Scrape batter into center of baking sheet. With damp hands, form into a log 8–10 inches long and 2 inches high. Bake for 25 minutes. Remove from oven and let cool. Slice at an angle when completely cool (otherwise it will crumble). Lay each piece flat on baking sheet and bake for another 10–15 minutes. Let cool on cooling rack.

COCONUT CREAM PARFAIT

2 servings

. . . .

Ingredients:

⅔   cup coconut cream (not milk)
¼   cup nondairy milk
½   teaspoon vanilla extract
10   drops liquid stevia
½   teaspoon sea salt
½   cup fresh berries of choice for garnish
¼   cup raw slivered almonds for garnish

Directions: In a food processor, blend the coconut cream, nondairy milk, vanilla, stevia, and sea salt until combined well. Chill in the refrigerator to firm up the pudding.

Place in a serving bowl or parfait glasses and top with fresh berries and slivered almonds.

Acknowledgments

....

I AM SO GRATEFUL TO MY TEAM, who continues to help me educate, inspire, and empower people to achieve optimal health and thrive. Alison Charbonneau, chef extraordinaire, for your creativity and inspiration—without you this book would not have become a reality. Bobak Radbin, for your beautiful photography, making each dish look so inviting. Patricia Spadaro, my executive editor, for your creative input and guidance, expert editing and oversight, and your support each step of the way. Janet Chaikin, for your superb editing. Nita Ybarra, for the beautifully designed cover and interior. Nigel Yorwerth, for your invaluable guidance, marketing, and great foreign rights representation. Irene Zaragoza, for being my right arm and loyal supporter and helping me to get it all done. Thank you as well for your beautiful pottery, which can be seen in many of the photos. Thank you, Mom, for being my biggest cheerleader and rock of support. And, especially, to my clients and readers who kept nudging and inspiring me to put out a cookbook—this is for you!

Index

Page references in italics refer to photographs

About the Author

....

ANN BOROCH IS A CERTIFIED nutritional consultant, naturopath, educator, award-winning author, and inspirational speaker. She specializes in allergies, autoimmune diseases, and gastrointestinal and endocrine disorders and is an expert on candida. Her successful practice in Los Angeles, California, has helped thousands of clients achieve optimum health.

Ann's passion is to help people realize that the body has an innate intelligence that allows it to heal itself—the key is to give it the right environment for a long enough period of time to remove inflammation and infection. She firmly believes that with choice and diligence, each of us has the power to overcome any challenge.

Her healing wisdom comes through hard-earned experience: Ann was diagnosed with multiple sclerosis at the age of twenty-four. Refusing to accept this devastating verdict, she educated herself about the real factors underlying her condition, created her own self-care program, and has been symptom free for over twenty years. She is now trained in several healing disciplines.

Ann Boroch is the author of the popular books *The Candida Cure: Yeast, Fungus, and Your Health—The 90-Day Program to Beat Candida and Restore Vibrant Health* and *Healing Multiple Sclerosis: Diet, Detox, and Nutritional Makeover for Total Recovery.*

To learn more about Ann Boroch and her work, visit www.annboroch.com
Email: contact@annboroch.com | Facebook: AnnBorochNaturopath | Twitter: @annboroch